They're Your Kids Not Your Friends

They're Your Kids Not Your Friends

Shirlee Smith

SORIN BOOKS   Notre Dame, IN

www.sorinbooks.com

International Standard Book Number: 1-893732-31-2

Cover design by Eric Walljasper

Text design by Brian C. Conley

Printed and bound in the United States of America.

Library of Congress Cataloging-in-Publication Data
Smith, Shirlee.
    They're your kids, not your friends / Shirlee Smith.
        p. cm.
ISBN 1-893732-31-2
1. Parenting--Anecdotes. 2. Parent and child--Anecdotes. I. Title.
    HQ755.8 .S633 2001
    649'.1--dc21
                                            2001002440
                                                    CIP

Contents

Introduction

In 1966, as a single parent on welfare, I decided to go back to school. I enrolled in Pasadena City College, a school designed to bridge high school and university. A year later I was selected to participate in the High Potential Program—a special program at UCLA. I studied sociology.

The required English 101 class at Pasadena City College was the kind of experience that kept most students from feeling good about themselves. As I look back, it wasn't so much the class as it was the teaching assistant, who as an advanced student was hired to read and grade papers. She constantly and consistently marked my essays with a C- or D+ as she scribbled the same note in the left-hand margin.

One of those papers, with a C-, was a detailed account of my discovery that one of my children had substituted the sugar in the sugar bowl with salt. TRITE, she scribbled across the left-hand margin. And in her usual manner, she had added, "You need to focus on the important things in life!"

I thought I was!

There is nothing trite about parenting.

So for more than twenty years now I have been writing about the "trite" stuff—about the important things in life that happen to common, everyday parents.

I have been writing about the convictions that have governed my own life as a low-income, single parent of five children. I have been determined to raise them to become responsible, productive citizens not caught up by the trappings of a society flaunting violence, materialism, and classism.

I challenge parents to examine their values.

As a foster parent to more than a dozen babies born to drug-addicted mothers, I understand the meaning of being our sister's keeper. I write about addicted infants and have written, in particular, about Brandi, my foster daughter—and for whom I am now court-appointed guardian—who at nine years old has been with me since her birth. I write about making room for one more.

I write about my conviction that too many young women are having babies without understanding the full range of a child's needs that they will have to meet.

Why do I write?

I write because as parents we need to voice our values, priorities, and opinions so others who read and hear them can examine their own.

I write because I believe parenting is more important than anything else we do, and while there are many small components that make up the bigger picture—none of them is trite.

The Village

BACK WHEN

A ride on the streetcar all over Los Angeles used to cost seven cents. We used to call all carbonated soda "Coke," and I remember being afraid to drink Dr. Pepper because it had a name too closely associated with medicine.

I also remember the day my elementary school teacher introduced the measurements of feet and yards. My experiences at that point in life, in relationship to feet and yards, covered only backyards and front ones, and for me feet were attached to legs.

How, I wondered, could feet and yards be used as a standard for measurement? Feet, I was sure, differed in size, and as I stood on the steps in my own backyard and looked into the neighbor's yards on either side, it was clear yards differed in size too.

There was no way, even if I were to take three giant steps in the "Mother May I?" game, that three of my feet would equal one yard. And even if they equaled out to the yard on my right, Mrs. Peterson's yard to the left was almost twice as big.

Back then when most of life was a constant puzzle and back then when nothing seemed to make much sense, there was one thing that stood clear. That one thing was my family's belief that children were to be taught a set of values, and those values were to be the cornerstone of our existence. The people we came into contact with had the same set of beliefs. All of this was part of everyone taking care of everyone else—and their children too.

My grandmother would tell a neighbor's child that she wasn't going to put up with their nonsense, and if they didn't straighten up she took charge.

Not only did my grandmother support the children-can-behave philosophy, but so did just about everyone else—from the butcher at the neighborhood market to the overweight lady who lived on the corner.

In those days everyone seemed to be everyone else's keeper, especially when it came to the young people. I never thought to call the butcher nosy when he told my mother I had been rude in giving him our order. I never thought to think of the fat lady on the corner as meddlesome when she informed my father that I was acting improperly as I passed her house on my way home from school.

As confused as I was about most other things in my environment, I did have it quite straight as to what was expected of me when it came to behavior.

The butcher and the fat lady didn't top my list of favorite people. In fact, most of the adults in my neighborhood, including my teachers and parents, didn't make the list of favorites. And of course, Mounge, my grandmother, could never have made the list of even possible considerations.

But one of the interesting things about back then was that the adults didn't care whether they were considered friend or foe. Back then adults knew they had a responsibility, and they carried it out with blatant disregard for popularity ratings.

The more I misbehaved on the street corner, the more often the fat lady called my mother. The more she called my mother, the more I disliked her. And the more I disliked her, the harder I tried to pretend I didn't see her when I passed her house and she was outside in her front yard.

But part of my proper behavior was to speak to adults and to be polite, so it didn't matter what I liked; there was a clear list of do's and don'ts, and whenever defiance set in (and it did quite often), there were a number of neighborhood people who put me back in line.

If I didn't speak to the fat lady because I pretended I didn't see her in the yard, my mother heard about that too.

A lot has changed since riding all over Los Angeles for seven cents, calling carbonated drinks "Coke," being afraid of Dr. Pepper, and not knowing how three feet could make a yard.

Now there's no yard for a fat lady to work in because apartments have been built on the old lots where houses used to stand. People live on different floors that have balconies facing the rear of the property, and when the occupants go out to water their plants that are in pots, they can't see any of the neighborhood children.

The kids can't be sent to pick up the meat order from the butcher at the corner store because it's been replaced by a supermarket located a mile from the house.

And the most important disappearance from the old neighborhood structure are those behavior codes our parents, grandparents, and everyone else we were in contact with made us adhere to.

WISDOM OF THE ELDERS

"Every shut eye ain't sleep," my stepfather always warned.

Country reasoning, I said to myself.

"Apples don't fall far from the tree," and, "Tell me who your friends are and I'll tell you who you are," were words from my mother's friend, and they always bothered me. Since apples never had anything to do with what was actually being discussed, that saying, like shut eye, was basically classified by me as just old folks' gibberish.

"What you put into life is what you get out," was one of my mother's nonsense statements.

And from her mother I always had to hear, "I've seen dogs obey so I know you children are going to do what I say."

My grandmother's commentary didn't get dumped in the pile of country reasoning or old folks' gibberish. Hers was plain ol' English.

I had seen dogs obey, and I knew this lady meant what she said about children because oft times I sported a few welts on my childhood legs that proved her determination.

I learned to mind, maybe not like the dogs who sit when they are told and who fetch the paper from the front lawn each morning, but I learned the values and traditions my family believed in. I grew from childhood to adolescence and no longer had welts that let me and others know the adults in my family meant business. I grew from adolescence to adulthood, and I learned to reason.

I discovered you get out of life what you put in. I discovered my mother's phrase wasn't nonsense after all. If you go to the bank with a friend each week and she makes a deposit in her account and you don't, when the two of you show up in a year or so to make a withdrawal, who will have something in her account?

Life, my mother said, was no different than the bank.

The country reasoning, the old folks' gibberish, and the nonsense preaching all became cornerstones of my existence. I later heard other people claim birds of a feather flock together, but I stuck with "show me who your friends are." I also came to understand apples and trees.

As a student at the University of California at Los Angeles I earned academic honors and studied under world-acclaimed professors, but without my background of nonsense country reasoning and old folks' gibberish, I would be uneducated, and worst of all, I would still believe every shut eye was, indeed, asleep.

SPARE THE SLIPPER

The old phrase "Spare the rod and spoil the child" wasn't a concept my father bought into. Not only did he ignore this notion—which was quite acceptable during the time in which I was raised—but whenever he was forced into dishing out corporal punishment, he flubbed his duty.

My childhood transgressions were usually handled by my mother—she didn't fool around.

I would have relished hearing her say, "Wait until your father comes home," because a spanking by Pops was something to look forward to.

On the only occasion I remember being hit by him, he used a felt slipper that belonged to his mother, Granny Pickett. First, he reluctantly held it in the air for me to see and then put it down on the front room couch where I sat frightened, not by the weight of the weapon that swayed and bent when he held it up, but more by the fact that my father was going to deliver the blows.

I can't remember what unacceptable behavior I had exhibited that brought the wrath of my parents upon me on that occasion, but having been a child, adolescent, and teenager who preferred to see life by my own standard, I'm quite positive I needed whatever punishment was to come my way.

Normally, when the time for recompense was upon me, I ran through the house or out the door into the yard begging for mercy. But there was a very different aura the day my father stood in front of me with the deep blue turquoise slipper that had yellow and pink flowers embroidered on the sides and red flowers across the top.

My fear was mixed with curiosity.

Granny Pickett's slippers didn't even make noise when she scooped through the house with them on. How in the world would it ever do the same job as the wooden hangers from the front hall closet my mother used, or how would it even come close to delivering the agony caused by the fresh switch I often had to pick from the tree out back?

Pops' voice was deep but kind. He was annoyed, but he didn't have the same "I'm not going to put up with your foolishness" kind of look my mother delivered on a daily basis.

Granny's slipper was a gentle experience, and some years later my father delivered another stellar performance.

My sixth-grade teacher, Mrs. Walker, at First Street Elementary School, said my attitude and behavior meant a parent would have to come and meet with her.

I was in agony, of course. My mother frequently met with the rulers of my childhood academia and the entire bunch of them, Mom included, made unreasonable allegations regarding my approach to life; and they always agreed upon an equally unreasonable solution to halt the way they saw me taking shape.

But on one fine early spring day, the front door of my classroom opened and my father stepped in, just over the threshold. Not all the way in. He quietly introduced himself to the teacher and asked Mrs. Walker to please step into the hallway. I was not called to join them.

The felt slipper incident had happened long before the sixth-grade one, and as I sat at my desk with the inkwell on the right-hand side, I wasn't thinking of the mild tap-tap Granny's footwear had produced. Instead, my heart was pounding very hard as I wondered when I would be called into the hallway.

Mrs. Walker came back into the classroom with a very, very red face. She treated me quite differently after her brief private chat with my father. Somewhere in the process of recognizing every child is different, my father understood I was not incorrigible but that I simply marched to a beat most adults didn't appreciate.

Wooden hangers and freshly picked switches played a very important role in keeping me in tow, but thanks to the few occasions when my father stepped in, I began to realize it was really quite okay not to be the perfect little person so many adults thought I should be.

Respect

Lily Pickett didn't have much of a chance with me—she was old. As far as I was concerned, she had always been that way. I thought she had been born old.

Granny Pickett's hair was never combed to hang down her back. She had a lot of it, but she wore it in a bun that seemed to grow from a special scalp on the back of her neck. As far as I knew, hair was just made on her head that way. And even worse, I believed her hair had always been that color.

My grandmother also wore clothes that looked odd, and they were always dull colors. Bright-colored items had no place in her wardrobe. From my earliest memories, she was someone I didn't understand.

I was also troubled by her unwavering need to adjust the folds in my cardigan sweaters to hang on my body just like her old-lady sweaters fit her. No matter where I was going, if she was anywhere near and I had on a sweater, she patted, tucked, and folded until it hung and looked the way hers did. Of course, as soon as I was out of sight I fixed my sweater to hang and fit in the fashion school-girls' sweaters were supposed to.

Another reason I knew Granny Pickett was ancient was because she never believed I was learning or had learned to read. She believed in reading to children, and at the foot of what I thought was a very ugly-looking (antique) rocking chair I probably heard every story written for young people.

My grandmother read me the funnies until I hated both Blondie and Dagwood. I learned not to like Sluggo or Nancy thanks to Granny Pickett and the resentful attitude I harbored but had sense enough never to express.

Did my grandmother's hair really need to blow in the wind and did she really need to wear bright colors for me to appreciate her?

Why didn't I realize my grandmother was someone very special in my life? Why didn't I appreciate all those times she took me to the movies?

I loved the movies, and back then little girls got dressed up with curls in their hair and white gloves on their hands to go to the picture show. Granny Pickett always had to change the way my mother had curled my hair; but one thing in my favor, she didn't put my hair in a bun.

Although I loved the movies and being pretty for the day, I was ashamed to be in the company of my grandmother, and that was simply because she was old and old wasn't something good.

Where did I get such a negative attitude? Was society to blame because I had a problem with my grandmother because she was old? Back then there were no televisions in the home, so I wasn't barraged with commercials focusing on youth and I never saw a magazine ad for anti-aging cream. Where did I get such an attitude?

Appreciation for the elderly has to begin at home. Although my parents told me I had to respect Granny Pickett and all the other adults and elders in our circle of friends and relatives, respect is more than a concept, and it must be developed by teaching the young the value and importance of the older generation.

MAKING ENDS MEET

Remember Scarlett in *Gone With the Wind* wearing the wonderful dress that was made from the lavish drapes that once covered the windows in her elegant mansion, Tara?

It probably wasn't seeing the movie and viewing Scarlett's dramatic decline from a southern lady of plenty to a destitute, resourceful one that set the tone for my own style of existence. The truth about my lifestyle is simply the age-old axiom, "Necessity is the mother of invention." And that's undoubtedly the same force that drove Scarlett to order her household slave to cut up her window drapes to make a marvelous velvet gown.

Before I heard of Tara, my mother and most of her friends had already surrounded me in an environment of survival strategies.

These ladies—my mother and most of her friends—were domestics; some were live-ins, some were day-workers, and others only went to the white folks' homes on Thursdays to do laundry. All of them were paid money to service the good life, but none of them was paid enough to live even a simple life.

I learned a lot about survival from all of them. There was the story about the goose that was cooked for dinner by the day-worker in Boston when she was only thirteen years old and had never seen a goose and, of course, knew nothing about cooking one. From that story the message was clear: you deliver when you're on the line. When in a tight spot, my mother's friends preached, "You call on every experience you've ever had and create, create, create!"

Unlike Prissy, who in *Gone With the Wind*, when the day of reckoning came, disappeared, and then finally admitted she knew nothing at all about "birthin' babies," the young girl in the goose story had never claimed she was a cook, nor did she have an opportunity to disappear or offer up an excuse. The young girl had been hired as a baby-sitter for a wealthy family, and when she arrived on the first day of work, the lady of the house immediately slipped into a fashionable coat, adjusted her expensive gloves on her dainty, slim fingers, and while closing the front door smiled and ordered the girl to have the goose prepared for the 5:30 p.m. evening meal.

My mother's "Lady's Home Survival Circle" met informally but frequently; sometime they met by twos and other times by threes—but always sitting around our kitchen table. They had a jam-packed agenda, but at my young age there was a lot I thought was downright silly. However, in later years the conversations which I remembered became guidelines for living.

My mother sewed, but, unlike at Scarlett's Tara, my parents' home never had any floor to ceiling windows with elegant velvet draperies. Instead, we had an abundance of good quality but out-of-style hand-me-down items.

My mother took many a lace collar and matching cuffs from one dress, ripped up another one, and removed the elegant buttons from still another to provide dresses for piano recitals and other special events.

As a little girl, I never appreciated this style of providing. But having six children of my own now, I am grateful to know how to change a discarded size 20 jumpsuit into several pairs of stylish summer shorts. I am grateful to know how to change the baked potatoes left from last night's dinner into hash browns for tomorrow morning's breakfast.

VILLAGE MOTHERS

There are lots of mothers I pay homage to. My biological one gets accolades for providing me with so many of them.

Alice Wilson, my mother's friend from when they were teenagers, guided me through the supermarket aisles during my early married years. She taught me to watch the weekly newspaper ads for specials. Without fail, every Thursday afternoon she pulled her car into my driveway and off we went to "make groceries" on Brooklyn Avenue in Boyle Heights, which is an East Los Angeles neighborhood.

Ms. Wilson lectured on the necessity of planning meals in advance and of shopping with a list. If I hadn't done my homework and couldn't produce a written plan, her car didn't move until I sat there and completed the task.

Ms. Wilson could stretch a dollar—and not just ones allocated for food.

"After October," she cautioned, "anything you're buying for the kids? Save it, wrap it, and put it under the Christmas tree in December."

Through regular conversations and informal counseling sessions, I learned many a formula from her that made my job as a homemaker and parent more manageable.

During one of our sessions she declared, "Always remember this: your children aren't your friends—they are your children."

Then there was Dolores Jones who decided to call me her own on the evening she visited my parents' home and I was on the back porch with a large knapsack, a loaf of freshly baked bread, and a battered violin case. I was running away because no one bought me the pair of skates I'd spotted in the Sears catalog.

Years later, when I was an adult, Ms. Jones and I had lot of laughs speculating on how far I would have gotten headed out of town going who-knows-where through the busy streets of Los Angeles.

Ms. Jones and I enjoyed some of those laughs during the endless hours we spent together soaking the cast off my infant daughter's legs. Pamela, my oldest, was born with club feet. At ten days old, she was released from the hospital with knee-high casts on both legs; they had to be changed every two weeks. The orthopedist preferred not to cut them because he said the baby was too young. So, Ms. Jones sat with me for hours soaking and peeling plaster.

Mary White, who my mother met when both their husbands were porters on the Southern Pacific Railroad long before I was born, sold me a house full of great furniture for only fifty cents. Well, maybe a little bit more than that, but what a bargain and what a great help she was.

Lorraine Laremore, the most fashionable of my mother's friends, was a fabulous seamstress who gave me yards of material and bundles of trim that I used to make fine fashions for my children.

Ida Harrison-Davis cried tears and begged my mother not to let me marry when I was engaged at the too-young age of fifteen.

And there are many more: Vabel Reid, Viola Lomack, Aunt Grace, Vera Gordon, Palma Lawrence, Beryl Wilson. I could keep on, but I have to stop somewhere.

No Celebration

As a little girl and also as a teenager, I always asked my mother what she would like as a gift for Mother's Day. Her answer was always disappointing.

Gifts, I believed back then, should be shopped for, wrapped in pretty packages, tied with streaming ribbons, and topped with elegant bows. Gifts, I believed, were to be presented in a manner of celebration with a pretty card attached and many "oohs" and "aahs" emanating from the recipient and any other present or future bystander or onlooker.

Much to my dismay, year after year, my mother's concept of a Mother's Day gift put a damper on my entire shopping and subsequent presentation effort. As I reflect back, I can't remember one elegant package I presented her with.

Oh, I'm sure, throughout the years I gave some ribbons and bows. But it's funny how my memory fails to contain even a shred of evidence to help me recollect what one of those presents might have been. Instead, my mother's repeated response as to what she would like to have blankets my memory.

My mother never changed. She never requested a coat or a coffee pot. She never asked for jewelry, and she never wanted to be taken out for dinner or be served breakfast in bed.

My mother, I used to think, took all the fun out of the special day. While my friends were exclaiming how pleased their moms would be with the gifts they were giving, I knew as I added my own gift item to the conversation that my enthusiasm was as contrived as the gift I claimed to have purchased.

Although my mother repeated her same request throughout the years, I never really heard her. I'm not sure I even believed her. When I became a teenager, I remember deciding she was playing the pitiful role of "please don't do anything special for me."

But finally one day I heard her. By then I had children of my own, and that's when I knew her answer had been one of deep meaning and sincerity. I realized my mother's request that I simply give her the gift of obedience and adherence to a value system that she attempted to instill was indeed the most important of all gifts any mother could ever receive.

Oh, the packages are a delight to receive. And their brilliant bows and elegant wrappings make the occasion festive. A special treat of breakfast in bed with flowers on the serving tray or dinner reservations helps to let mothers know it's their day. But to see our children leading productive lives and adhering to a value system that has been part of the family's tradition for generations is, I realize, the best gift of all. Only after I became a mother did I understand.

WAIT 'TIL YOU GROW UP

My mother was always funny—even when she was being very serious. My mother was funny, all right, but she never made me laugh.

My mother was funny because she was so ridiculous. She was ridiculous because she had so many outrageous rules, goals, and expectations.

"How come the other kids don't have to give their mother a telephone number of where they're going to be?" I always wanted to know.

"I don't know the address of the party, I just know where the house is, so how can I tell it to you before I leave?" was my weekend argument that never got me out the front door.

"Why can't the guy blow his horn and then I run out and get into his car?" "Why do you have to meet these people before I can date them?" "What difference does it make if I have company when you're not home?"

Her answer to any and all of my teenage dilemmas was always the same—"I know I'm ridiculous and unreasonable, but all you have to do is be just a little patient. You'll grow up and have a little girl of your own, and then you won't be like I am and you can let her do all of the things I didn't let you do."

When she delivered these lines, she usually had a faint smile on her face. Once in a fit of teenage rage, I asked her why she thought she was so funny. Humor, she said, is strictly in the attitude of the situation. What's funny, she said, is in the delivery and in the acceptance.

With her right index finger making syncopated motions in my face, with her left hand ungraciously propped on her left hip, her stern lips parted on a face that lost its faint smile, she asked, "DO you think I'm trying to be funny?"

Like all teenagers, I thought I was pretty clever, and a large part of teenage cleverness is that they think their parents are pretty dumb—especially their mothers with those soft feminine voices.

I went for the voice and ignored her tone of delivery. I ignored the attitude of the situation, and more important, I ignored my mother's body language, including the syncopated motions of the right index finger.

I was dressed for the party. She knew my date who was already sitting in the living room waiting for me. He hadn't blown his horn; he had knocked on the front door. He had met her criteria. What did she mean, I wasn't going to the party because I had violated curfew the last time I was out? Surely she was joking, and yes, I wanted to know why she thought she was so funny.

My date heard the sting—the one I felt delivered upside my head by my mother's index finger accompanied by the rest of the fingers and the palm of her right hand.

My mother may have had a soft voice, but she also had a stinging right hand for any of her children who thought they knew it all.

It's a long time now since she was in her prime. I didn't think she was funny back then, but we sure have lots of laughs about her now.

Although I wasn't too patient, just as Mom foresaw, I had little girls of my own—five to be exact. It was only after I had them that I fully understood that smile my mother always had when she delivered those outrageous and ridiculous rules I had to abide by.

I don't know whether I had her same smile when I checked the driver's license of the young men who dated my daughters, or when I had to act out the other outrageous responsibilities of a parent. When my kids were growing up they didn't think I was too funny either, but now that they're grown we sure have lots of laughs.

One of the biggest joys of parenthood is finding the humor.

Children of My Own

THE GOOD DIE YOUNG

The year was 1959. The baby wasn't quite two years old. It was summertime, and it happened during one of the unbearable heat spells that come to Southern California.

My little one was plump and cuddly. She was an adorable little girl, and just before dinner that evening she and her sister, who was one year older, had gotten a special treat—a shower in the lawn sprinkler to cool them off for the evening.

Even though the night didn't bring much of a break in the heat, both the girls slept well.

Breakfast the next morning found the youngsters chattering at the table, as usual. But the chattering soon came to a halt and the events that followed changed the pattern of our household forever.

"Paula's playing with her food and won't chew it," three-year-old Pamela reported. I stopped eating, looked across the table, and gently reminded the baby not to keep stuffing food into her mouth, but to chew up what was already there.

Three-year-olds love to give reports, and immediately following the first announcement, Paula's behavior was again called to my attention by her sister Pamela. This time, though, the baby was being reported on for spitting out her food.

By the time I looked at her, Paula had lost control of everything—she couldn't even hold her spoon. Her eyes had a strange and distant glassy stare. And it was true, she could no longer keep the food in her mouth.

The pediatrician who immediately was called believed it was too severe an occurrence for an office visit and recommended we take her directly to the hospital emergency room.

It was a full day of doctors and testing, but there were no answers. And by the end of the day, the same little girl, who had lost her ability to walk, talk, focus, or perform any functions, was able to master all of them. Paula appeared perfectly normal. She sat up on the hospital table and told me she was hungry. She got down and ran around the floor.

The doctors said there was nothing wrong and sent her home. I didn't agree and the following day went to see her pediatrician. On that day, she cried when her leg was touched. She didn't want to play; she just sat around very, very quietly.

The pediatrician had Paula admitted to the hospital for extensive testing. In a week we were told that her lab work was being sent to Atlanta, Georgia, to a research center that was studying a disease no one else knew very much about. The results came back—my little girl had sickle cell disease.

Like others, we had never heard of the disease—but we learned. Paula's inability to function that morning at the breakfast table was explained to us as a sickle cell crisis that may have been brought on by having been chilled by the shower in the lawn sprinkler the night before.

Paula stayed in the hospital for two weeks, and when she left she wore a brace on her left leg because a nerve had been damaged as a result of the crisis.

Paula wore her brace and went to therapy, and she was wonderfully well for two more months; then she experienced a series of crises which left in her in a coma. She remained in the hospital for several months and died shortly after her second birthday.

What does a parent say to the other children about the baby who is never going to come back home?

Death is seldom easy, and sometimes having to talk about it is even harder. But no matter the difficulty of the experience, there were wonderful, special quiet times that allowed me personal reflections of the young life that so quietly passed away.

The death of a child is devastating, but learning to question those in the medical profession—not to simply agree with them when they say that things are fine because they appear that way for a brief moment, but to get a second opinion—is crucial when it comes to parents providing care for their children.

IDENTITY CRISIS

Getting Pamela to stop crying that day was the most difficult job I've ever had. Sitting there in front of her television, she was quite perplexed by the large number of black people on the screen and the emotions that were being expressed. Pamela was also perplexed by the emotions of the speaker, and she was puzzled by the message.

Romper Room, Sheriff John, cartoons, and other kiddie programs of her television world had not been any preparation for this kind of human event coverage. She didn't know what to make of it.

America hadn't experienced anything quite like it either. And reports from those who were part of that great march on Washington say it was, indeed, a once-in-a-lifetime experience.

Pamela is in her forties now, and she has only recently stopped crying. Oh, back then we managed to wipe away her childhood tears, but her cry wasn't something to be handled with tissues, for it wasn't one that mommies or daddies can make disappear with soft, reassuring words.

By now, my Pamela has come to discover there is pride in being black. But back in 1960, when she listened to Martin Luther King and when she watched great hordes of black people assembled at the Lincoln Monument, she didn't know who she was.

When I answered her "why," by telling her briefly of the Negro struggles in this country, she wanted to know what that had to do with her. She said she wasn't a Negro and she cried dramatically when I wouldn't agree with her. It didn't help the situation when she asked her father to see her point of view. She was a Negro—a colored person—just like the people in the crowd on her TV screen. And she was told that she and her entire family and a large portion of their friends were all part of the discrimination and segregation Dr. King was so eloquently presenting.

Pamela was too young to comprehend America's racial divide or the new wave of dedication to eradicate it. But she wasn't too young to have internalized negative feelings about her color.

Pamela had all the proper children's books on her shelf. She'd heard all the fairy stories and she'd heard all the nursery rhymes.

Pamela had her own record player and her kiddie collection covered what every little girl under eight years old should have.

We took her to the museum and she attended local theater productions. She was enrolled in a dance class and she went to the library regularly. She also attended arts and craft class.

However, *Parents* magazine and the other proper authorities of that time period neglected to remember there was a Negro population that had a separate and defined set of needs.

As I watched the sea of dark and light faces at the monument that day, I listened intently to Martin Luther King's words, and as I wiped at my little girls' tears, I realized how deep the Americanization process has scarred people of color.

Without a focus on our struggles and without the demand for holidays, African-American studies, and other programs that focus on the contributions and achievements of black people, individually and collectively, we will still have little children crying and parents without the tools of assurance to soothe them.

A BARGAIN SHOPPER

For one whole year my daughter Pia searched for the perfect pair of dressy shoes. When she finally found a pair at the mall, she asked me to go back to the store with her to see if the shoes looked good on her very narrow feet and, of course, to have me write the check.

By the time she put the shoes on and walked across the showroom floor, the smile she had started with began to sour. "Mom," she complained, "don't you think these gap right here in the middle?"

I looked for the space, but before I could find it or answer her question she found another problem with the fit. Her dissatisfaction continued to mount, and although she continued to ask for my opinion, her questions were rhetorical.

Throughout the year she found other shoes which she knew were just the ones. The scene at the first store was repeated many times.

Finally there was a breakthrough. My wonderful Pia had a friend with a pair of shoes with "the look" she wanted. We dashed to the shoe store, but alas, her size was not in stock, and even after a delivery to the store of more shoes the following week, there were none to fit Pia.

Is this a complaint about Picky Pia? Not hardly, because her shoe money became the monthly whatever-comes-up fund. One month it was used for a car battery, the next month for a dentist bill, and so the story went. Or, let's say, so the cash went.

I have no complaints. My girl's shopping habits were what many a mom might dream of. She's picky and she always hunts for a bargain.

Well, now, I must be honest: there were lots of things on the shoe store and department store shelves that made Pia's young eyes sparkle. And I suppose if the end of the month bank statement didn't have to balance our deposits with our withdrawals in the checkbook, the picture of the expensive all-leather boots she had plastered on her bedroom wall just might have materialized into a purchase—provided they came in extra narrow width.

It probably would have been safe to buy them even though they cost five times more than I could afford, because Pia would have changed her mind shortly after she got them home and returned them. It was wonderful living with Pia—she was great for the household budget.

FUR-LINED HANDCUFFS

My oldest daughter, Pamela, is naive. Only now has she begun to understand, even though she's an adult, that various situations call for specific kinds of behavior.

As her mother, I suppose I shouldn't complain, because what she generally displays is a fairly good set of manners. And I never taught any lessons that said to abandon polite behavior if you get arrested and go to jail.

So when she was pulled over for outstanding traffic warrants and hauled off to spend the night in lock-up, her "good morning" greetings to her cellmates the following morning got her, in return, a barrage of curse words.

What's that about when in Rome? She should have held her greeting and watched what others did when they rolled off their nighttime cots.

But Pamela was out of it from the very beginning. When the officers took her to the side of the road, she complained to them that she was going into shock when they announced she would be taken to the station and booked.

In telling the story to the family, she said she was quite impressed with the consideration the officers had shown her on the ride to the station. Living in the 'hood, we were all ears for this very different kind of story. After all, this was the infamous Los Angeles Police Department we were about to hear something good about.

After crying when the handcuffs were clamped on and while complaining about the roughness of the metal against her tender young wrist, Pamela said the officers were able to calm her tears by explaining recent decisions made at the station.

"The department has on order new handcuffs that are fur-lined," she said with the look and attitude of a true believer.

Poor Pamela.

But she's wiser now. Although she only spent one night in the slammer, a few additional experiences have shown her why her cellmates didn't think the morning was good and why the arresting officers would make fun of her complaints about uncomfortable handcuffs.

Here's another story:

Visiting hours at the jail facility, she was told, were from 6 p.m. to 9 p.m., so she arrived there at 8:30 p.m. to visit an inmate—her boyfriend. She found out she was too late to be processed.

She went back the next day and stood in line for an hour and went through the process which included producing valid identification. For Pamela and most everyone else in line the ID was a driver's license.

"Mommie," she said indignantly as she told the tale, "I didn't want to believe it, but I saw for myself. While visitors were being processed, their driver's license numbers must have been entered into the computer because after we had gotten into the glassed-in area, and were talking by telephone to the inmates, three people (visitors) were pulled aside and arrested."

Pamela says she saw officers approach a visitor who was on the telephone near her, and she says she heard him being told he was under arrest. He was then moved to a separate area.

Lessons to be learned here: When you teach your children good manners, tell them there are some places they might not want to use them. Remind them that unpaid traffic tickets can land them in the slammer. And last, but very important, if they want to visit a boyfriend, buddy, or relative in jail, tell them to stay away if the long arm of the law is looking for them for any kind of reason.

LOW INCOME
DOESN'T EQUAL POVERTY

Nowadays, supermarket aisles are being blocked with slow-moving shoppers carefully scrutinizing various sized grocery lists, and this isn't just the story at the discount market. Even at the ritzy markets where the Cadillacs, Jaguars, and Mercedes line the parking lots, their classy owners are inside selecting items on their prepared lists of needs, and well-heeled people are seen counting out their money-saving coupons upon arriving at the checkout counter.

It seems almost everybody is watching where the dollars go these days. And it's strange to discover all these people utilizing the tricks for survival that many of us have been using all our lives.

As a mother of five children on a very measured income (welfare), if it wasn't an essential item, it didn't get into my grocery cart. For years, I would look into other carts that were nearby in the checkout line and I would wonder about the giant-sized potato chip packages, commercially-made syrups, packages of candy, and other items that fell into the foreign food category when it came to living at my house.

I was still making potato chips by shaving the Idahos or russets I purchased at the discount vegetable market, and I was still making my syrup by measuring twice the amount of sugar as the water boiling on the stove. A bit of maple flavoring and the recipe was ready for hot cakes or waffles. There was no candy, and maybe that was partly the reason the children never had cavities.

Did I shop that way because I didn't have much money, or was it because I believed in purchasing only what was essential? I could have spent twice as much on groceries, but then I would have had less to spend on other items.

Back then I didn't have much money, and government food stamps certainly didn't stretch very far. I shopped the way I did because I wouldn't have made it any other way.

But what happened when I had an income of my own? I didn't shop with a list, not because I didn't believe in them, but because I was already programmed for what to pull off the shelf.

Living on a low-income budget doesn't necessarily mean you're poor. Poverty is a way of thinking, and making a grocery list and sticking to it is a step in the direction of upward mobility. Learning to live with a small amount of money is excellent preparation for the time when there's more.

Puttin' Food on the Table

As I stuffed the 89-cent per pound string beans into the plastic bag, the lady next to me at the discount vegetable store commented that she had heard they were selling for $1.19 a pound at the supermarket.

"Well," she said, "with the price of things, I think our kids will soon learn to be appreciative—they've had it too good for too long."

She went on to say she remembered the day, when she was young, that no one asked what was for dinner. The big question back then, she said, was whether there would be any dinner.

Yes, our children have grown up to be unappreciative. They really don't know what it is to be without. My own used to tell me when I talked about starvation in the world that they would donate the nasty liver on their plate and they would gladly pay the refrigerated transportation cost to ship it overseas.

Mine, not unlike other young people where we lived, constantly complained about meals. They reminded their parents that they had what was being served just three days ago and something just like it the week before. Our children want this and they want that. Some older folk remember eating oatmeal for days at a time, three times a day.

The other day I was in line behind a young boy who purchased about four bucks worth of snack pies, potato chips, candy, gum, and soft drinks. Four dollars down the drain. Not one of his purchases had any needed nutrients. What kind of money-spending guidance has he been given?

Stretching the dollar dictates practical behavior, and that doesn't mean letting children determine what goes into the shopping cart.

Those who believe their children should grow up under better circumstances than they did may come to realize that the struggles they endured are what made them strong. On the surface there is nothing wrong with the concept of a better life for our young; but what has happened underneath that surface is we have raised some very spoiled, non-suffering brats who think life should be a bed of roses. That includes eating whenever they want and only what their taste buds tell them they want.

Let the little ones miss meals a few times when they won't eat this and can't eat that, and they will learn to eat what's on the table. Give the teenagers the week's food money and let them plan the menus and do the shopping and the preparing, and they will learn to appreciate what goes into putting food on the table.

Sound harsh? Raising kids is no simple task and allowing them to believe meals are their choice even when they're at home—and not looking at the McDonald's drive-thru menu—is keeping them from recognizing that meals and food aren't guaranteed.

EDDIE MURPHY WASN'T FUNNY

If analyzed well, the errors we make while traveling life's highways can often be turned into great lessons for improvement and future success. I made a big one, and I'm now confessing, analyzing, and cleansing my soul.

If anyone were to ask me about movie ratings, I would certainly have responded that I knew what they were and how they worked. I would have said something like "G" movies were for the general public—the entire family. I would have given *Bambi* and other Disney-type films as examples. Movies about animals would more than likely be lumped into this category.

"PG"? My answer would suggest the rating was for films with a little parental guidance suggested. Maybe even a Disney could fit in here.

And the films with "R" ratings were for those over seventeen years of age. An "R" rated film was one with more bad language, a few killings with blood, and a few sex scenes.

Films with an "X" rating were something I never even bothered to think about because I wasn't going to see them.

My kids had a fairly good handle on what kind of film they would have permission to see. But I didn't stay awake on the job. Still assigned to me, under the category of home responsibilities, was one minor child under the age of eighteen.

She was fifteen, and I was still responsible for calling the shots, even the ones that seemed quite minor, like what movies are good entertainment and appropriate to see.

I didn't realize I had abandoned my responsibility until the fourth person was killed by close-range gunshots on the movie screen which was projecting the film my fifteen-year-old had selected for us to see because she heard it was funny.

She had told me it was an "R" movie, but when asked how it qualified, she said it was because of the language.

I could handle that, and this guy Eddie Murphy, whom she loved from *Saturday Night Live*, was going to peddle his comedic talents on the big screen.

There were some funny scenes, and Murphy had some funny lines. But before I got to see Murphy and be amused, two prison guards had been shot dead in the first few opening minutes; two detectives were thereafter splattered in the hallway and lobby of a hotel; and another body with a bullet hole in the head was laid out on a park bench.

Between the women prostitutes in the film being at the mercy of men, as abducted girlfriends or just women eager for a quickie, and the handsome Native American who was a crazed killer, I had difficulty laughing with Murphy.

My daughter was right: there was profanity. But since I can tolerate some foul language and since I didn't feel her young ears had been spared introduction to language she wasn't permitted to use, I didn't let profanity be the sole criteria for eliminating a movie from our list.

I'm glad I made the error because I went home and did some homework on updating my knowledge of the rating system. And seeing the film together made for a good discussion regarding violence and the depiction of minorities and women in film. It also gave my daughter the opportunity to hear my lecture about the under-ten-year-olds who were in the theater with their parents.

Parenting is a forever-learning experience not to ever be confused with knowing it all.

Not in This House!

When the babies had diaper rash, the old folk advised corn-starch. When the little ones grew older and started losing teeth, the old folk had advice for that too.

And then there were the lessons about raising children that I learned from my own experiences growing up. I didn't always have to ask for advice.

But the day I was invited into my teenage daughter's bedroom to share in her admiration of a new wall-sized poster of her rock idol, Prince, I realized neither the old folk nor my own experiences had prepared me for the '80s.

"He isn't nude," she protested in her usual temperamental you-don't-understand-anything manner. No, he wasn't quite nude. But he was nude! It was the first time in twenty-seven years of address-ing parenting or household issues that I used the line, and I stam-mered while delivering it: "This is a Christian household," I said in desperation.

What Christianity had to do with Prince or what I thought it had to do with him I'll probably never know. Maybe it was the fail-ure of the old folk reasoning to prepare me for the poster or maybe it was my own growing up experience with pictures of Nat King Cole—fully dressed—that brought me to call on a higher being.

I'm no prude. I've seen nudity. I've seen pictures of nude peo-ple. But the Prince poster? This man, as my daughter so aptly point-ed out, wasn't nude. He wasn't actually without anything on, but he was standing in a shower with only a few beads of water and a G-string on. For matters of description he was nude; it was also the come-hither look on his face.

The poster was taken off the wall. But the wonderful tunes on Prince albums owned by my daughter continued to fill our house with mellow music and a good beat. I was happy to pat my foot and snap my fingers to his music. From time to time I could even understand some of his lyrics. Well, actually, only a word or two.

Prince's music became so enjoyable I was doing my morning exercises to his tune "1999." I couldn't understand most of the lyrics, but I did manage to catch something addressed to President Reagan that went something like, "Ronnie talk to Russia before it's too late. Ronnie talk to Russia before they blow up the world."

A man of substance, I said to myself as I began the leg lift routine. My girl Peggy had good taste. I even remembered an interview in a magazine she had shown me where Prince was talking about his heroes being people involved with social issues.

For weeks, I puffed and perspired through my morning paces while listening but being unable to discern what the guy was actually crooning about.

The words didn't really matter because Prince was a social activist. He was okay even though his poster wasn't.

I had understood the words to the song when I was young and heard Nat King Cole croon "Unforgettable." When I was a young adult, I was able to understand Otis Redding when he sang "On the Dock of the Bay," and I'd never had to figure out anything I'd heard from my country-western favorite, Charley Pride.

But the morning came when I learned Prince didn't sing about the same things King Cole did. That same morning I came to realize my daughter wasn't listening to the kind of troubles Otis Redding chronicled while sitting on the Dock of the Bay.

And while I'd been quite happy bending and stretching to my favorite of Prince's tunes, "Little Red Corvette," I wasn't too pleased to discover his Saturday night ride wasn't about a ride in the car at all. The lyrics quite clearly, once I got the hang of the style of delivery, actually described the kind of ride Prince was enjoying with a girl in the back seat of his daddy's car.

Nobody told parents that lyrics in the '80s weren't like lyrics in the '50s. How come Prince could market sex and not be rated "R"?

The cadre of older folks who had always been on hand to offer advice for my household simply shrugged their shoulders when I told them about Prince, and they also mumbled something about cornstarch clearing away diaper rash, but they never said it could do any thing for social ills.

TALKING BACK

A few days after my column about Prince ran in the newspaper, I picked up the editorial page and found the following letter to the editor. People who are moved by passion will respond quickly; this was quick! I'm always glad to get feedback and the letter was fascinating. The biggest fascination came when I read the signature. The letter was from my daughter, who was the owner of the Prince poster. It was signed Peggy Smith with no further identification!

In your recent article on Prince, you said after realizing what he was singing you indicated you were in shock.

I think if you look deeper into the lyrics of his songs you will understand more about young people's lives in the '80s.

If you look at TV programs, commercials, billboards, songs on every radio station, and news items on TV and radio and in newspapers, what do you see?

Sex.

It's sold to everyone, with no regard to age. Hair products, clothes, perfume—it seems as if everything has a deeper message: use this product and you'll be sexy. Sexy ads are no longer only available to those 21 and over. Everybody sees them.

Why jump all over Prince for an occasional song of sex that has the same meaning as commercials? At least he's open about it, and what's wrong with a person who says how he feels? The only difference between Prince's '80s music and your '50s music lyrics is that Prince is more to the point and up-front. I remember Rosemary Clooney and "Come on-a My House."

Beyond the sex Prince sings about are the social and human kind of issues. He sings about what's going on in the world and what is happening around him. He sings about D-day and world destruction. That day will be here, believe it or not, Prince says.

Prince also says, "I don't want people to get the impression that sex is all I write and sing about because it's not, and the reason it's so abundant in my writing is mainly because of my age and the things that are around me. Until you can go to college or get a 9–5 job, then there's going to be a bunch of free time around you—but if people don't dig my music, then stay away from it. That's all. It's not for everybody. But I do know that there are a lot of people who want to be themselves out there."

You have to understand that not everybody was brought up in the same lifestyle as you. Take note that Prince is also not from your generation. If Prince is to be rated "R" and banned, so should TV news stories on rape, sexy commercials, etc. But he shouldn't be banned—this is what his life is. It's what's happening, and you can't just ban some things and not ban others.

Yes, it's rotten what the world has come to, but the once small sore is now a cancerous disease, and it will take more than banning Prince and other products (or using cornstarch) to cure the spoiled society.

Also, spend another day exercising to Prince, read about him, try to understand where he's coming from. Next time, don't just write your article when you've done only half the research.

How Do They
Know So Much?

Once upon a time, I used Arm & Hammer detergent to wash my clothes. Then my daughter, Phoenix, dropped by the house and said, "Hmmmmm, this laundry doesn't have the clean fresh smell of Tide."

She said the stuff—and that's what she called it—I was using just didn't do what Tide could.

Ms. Laundry then conferred with her older sister Pamela regarding my inability to know and use a good product. The two made several cutting remarks about clothing items that were supposed to be clean but that were both dingy and without an aroma that said somebody really cared.

What nerve!

"Don't you remember," Phoenix reminisced, "the time at the laundromat when mom was stuffing too many clothes into the machine and I told her they wouldn't get clean? Do you remember her reply?" she asked the older one.

"'I'm not here to get the clothes clean,' Mom said that morning while stuffing, and then she added the clincher, 'I'm simply here to wash them.'"

Yes, I did say that and meant every word!

Of course, clean clothes are sort of important, but that didn't make any difference. There's a point during information exchanges with my daughters when it's necessary to act crazy, irresponsible, and unpredictable.

This kind of behavior is required when their knowledge rises above the needs of the situation.

Like the time when Phoenix, the one with the degree from the University of California at Irvine, told me a word I'd used didn't exist.

"You meant to say 'enclave' not 'conclave,'" she said.

As we talked, she was sitting there checking her most current edition of Webster's New Collegiate Dictionary.

"Oh," she exclaimed in a tone filled with shock and disbelief. "You were right."

As parents, we don't hear that phrase too often. There isn't much for us to be right about anymore. Thank God for Webster!

Life is moving so swiftly, things are changing so rapidly, and new products are hitting the market so frequently, if it weren't for our little know-it-alls a lot of us would still believe the tea kettle was the fastest way to make a cup of hot tea.

"A microwave?" I inquired suspiciously.

"Put the thing in your room," I demanded when my daughter Pia moved back home and brought one with her.

"I think you might enjoy using it, if I show you how," she suggested mildly.

"I've gotten along quite fine without one for all these years, thank you," I responded. I said it in much the same way my grandmother probably did when my mother presented her with an iron that had an electrical cord and plug attached to it.

It's an endless saga that goes from generation to generation. But knowing that doesn't make it one bit easier to live with.

There was also the time the information from the high school drivers' education class took over my drive-time hours. Whenever the high school daughters, Peggy and Pia, were in the vehicle, as they began calling the car, they recited items from the California Driver's Handbook, which their instructor must have insisted they memorize in its entirety. This drive-time behavior of theirs wasn't preparation for their day at the wheel, as it might on the surface seem to suggest; it was simply a steady stream of calling attention to my minor (and major) driving infractions.

Depending on their age and their social environment, children will always have some kind of advice for parents, in part, because they are so impressed with all they think they know. Some of their information is quite useful. As parents, it's our job to determine what to fly with and what to leave in the hangar.

Love for One More—Foster Care

ROOM FOR ONE MORE

I once told someone my favorite pastime was sitting on the beach and watching the sunset.

"Yeah, I'm sure," was the sarcastic reply.

Another time I took a chance and told someone else about tears filling my eyes when I heard the details of a human interest story everyone was talking about.

This listener was harsher than the first one. "Shirlee Smith," he said, "tears in your eyes? Who do you think you're kidding?"

My confidant continued, "You just don't impress me as a woman with emotions. You're tough and hard-boiled. You don't give a damn about very much in life, so what's all this talk about tears in your eyes? I'm no pushover—so tell it to someone else."

What kind of image have I created?

Honestly, my favorite pastime is watching the sunset on the pier at Santa Monica Beach, but I go there all alone. I have tears in my eyes so often I usually don't wear mascara. When I'm in public and dab at my eyes with a handkerchief, people suspect there's some kind of environmental irritant.

So I guess I shouldn't have been surprised when a close friend said to me, "I don't believe it. You, caring for someone's new baby? You're supposed to be a woman on the go. What are you telling me?"

Even though I am the mother of six children, as a community activist I didn't come on the scene until my children were grown up. Most people never saw me with a baby or imagined, I now realized, that I ever had any babies—just teenagers and young adults.

But now I had what the Department of Children and Families called a newborn. And people who thought they knew me just didn't believe it was the real me.

People kept asking, "Are you kidding?"

At the time of life when I had no parental responsibilities (all my children were grown up and moved away) and at the time in life when time was my time, why?

Here's the reason: Every time a news program hits my television screen with a police bust and small children being hurried away to a waiting car by law enforcement authorities, tears swell up in my eyes. Every time a public service announcement heralds the need for foster parents, my thoughts of tranquillity at the seashore watching the sunset are shattered.

I'd always wondered how the folks with summer homes and winter lodges feel about their places standing empty when they knew there are people roaming the streets without shelter.

Instead of wondering about the rich folks, I instead decided to make my own contribution by using the bedrooms I had empty in my home, since my own children no longer occupied them.

While it is true that I am tough and, yes, even a little hard-boiled, I like to believe I am also socially responsible. Making room for one more child in my life in a society where too many little ones have been removed from parents, most times because they are incapable of providing adequate care, was quite simply *just the right thing to do.*

THE CIRCLE OF LIFE

Sometimes Brandi's questions turn to theories.

"Where did Granma Smiley go?" she asked just as soon as she was told my mother had passed away.

Before I could supply my well-prepared parental response, Brandi set forth her own calculation.

"Just like Mufasa in *The Lion King*, Granma's in heaven."

"Will she speak to me from the sky like Mufasa talked to Simba?" Brandi wanted to know.

I waited. She was waiting for me because for this one she didn't have her own answer/theory (or so I thought).

"Mom, is she going to talk to me from the sky? When can I look in a pool and see her face?" (In the movie Simba went to drink water and saw his dead father's reflection.)

"Mom, I can be Simba and run far away, just like he did in the movie when his father died."

Brandi was on a roll and seemingly prepared to relive the entire Lion King story, non-stop.

Mufasa's reflection in the pool and his talking from the sky seemed, to me, to be my best shot for our transition back to reality.

I said to her, as Rafiki, the wise baboon in this favorite story of hers was fond of saying, "It is time."

"Words of wisdom that the old folks leave us with will always be there, Brandi. We just have to be quiet and listen and pay attention."

I didn't tell Brandi, but my mother used to take special pleasure in reminding me that I am not in charge.

Mom frequently made a Shirlee Annette telephone call when there was a sudden change in the weather and she knew my plans for the day were related to the condition in the sky—a picnic and rain was falling.

"A higher being?" my mother would ask with a tinge of well-well-well.

"Granma Smiley said I was a lovely girl," Brandi replied. "Will she tell me that again, if I'm quiet?" (If I answered this question correctly that ride in the car to school each morning might have a lot less conversation about the cars with drivers who don't drive correctly and the benefits of taking one street versus another.)

I wished for just a small amount of time to think through this "Lion King" scenario that was unfolding too quickly.

I couldn't catch my thoughts, and Brandi had by now pulled out her stack of recycled paper and a box of crayons and was sketching clouds and images floating around in them.

"Yo, what's up?" I asked as she changed back and forth from one crayon to another.

"Here's a circle of life and over here is the baby and they are in the cloud with the circle and then here comes Granma Smiley over here. Sometimes people die and sometimes people are born. And sometimes lions die and sometimes lions are born and sometimes flowers die and sometimes we have to plant seed and my butterfly died because the wing was broken and it couldn't fly to find food and I didn't know how to feed it and. . . ."

She could have kept on going with her Brandi theory of life and death, but I thought it might be a good idea if we transitioned back to our talk about silence and giving Granma Smiley a chance to speak from the sky.

"Oh," said Brandi, when I brought back that part of the conversation. "I don't want to talk to her now, she just died and needs to rest. It's okay to die because it's just okay and then we can see their reflection in the water, maybe in the bathtub if there's no bubbles."

Maybe I shouldn't have interrupted, but I needed just a little silence. It isn't an everyday occurrence to lose one's mother.

"I miss my mother and I am sad and I need to be very quiet," I said.

"I can be very still, but I can hug you and I can be your mother too," Brandi said with an overwhelming amount of feeling and sincerity as she threw her arms around my body. What a wonderful little chatterbox.

DRUG BABIES:
PRISONERS OF WAR

A couple of billboards appeared on the main street near my house. They both showed a newborn baby with a variety of tubes and other life support equipment attached to its tiny and very frail young body.

The words on this public service eye-catcher announced in very blunt words, "He couldn't take the hit. If you're pregnant, don't use drugs."

The view of the emaciated, drug-addicted infant was chilling. When the traffic light turned from red to green, a lot of motorists took off a lot slower than usual. "But who pays attention to these 'Just Say No' messages?" someone asked when conversation centered around the disturbing picture and message seen on the billboard.

"Pregnant women don't see it and decide to start saying no to drugs," this person continued and went on to add, "Addicted women who might see the message, just like so many others sent their way, find nothing in the picture or in the words to cure their habit."

Of course this person was right!

The national war on drugs has been lost. Unfortunately, the biggest tragedy from this unfought war are the addicted babies whose lives will never be quite normal.

The life-support paraphernalia and the intensive care unit at the hospital are just the first steps in a life that will be filled with lab tests, therapists, neurologists, special education classes, evaluators, and psychologists.

All of this considered, the little ones are great, but most people don't seem to know that. I am a foster parent for special needs children—crack babies, to be exact. I've cared for twelve of them.

Time and time again I hear the same comment from people when they meet my babies: "They are darling. They are too cute. They're lovely. Are you sure something's the matter with them?"

Too many people think the birth mom's cocaine use is stamped on the forehead of her offspring. Too many people think babies and toddlers whose brain functions have been short-circuited by drugs should look deformed.

My babies are adorable—most little babies are. They're lovely, but most little ones are who have an organized schedule, plenty of rest, proper nutrition, lots of love, and a peaceful, quiet environment.

But lots of somethings *are* the matter with my babies—all of them. One of them, at two years old, didn't know how to play with toys. She had only just learned to wave good-bye. Her body was very stiff and her development was extremely delayed.

Another of the babies was described by the psychologist as extremely disorganized as evidenced in part by his extremely troubled sleep patterns. This little one had an outrageous temper, but he also has very thick, straight, long black eyelashes. He has great big beautiful brown eyes, and he knew how to make them twinkle, which made everyone who saw him break into a big broad smile.

Maybe the message on the billboard was for people who don't take drugs. Maybe the message was for people who know a life support system is really much more than tubes and other contraptions found in the hospital.

"If you're pregnant, don't take drugs" probably doesn't, as the person suggested, send a message to the addict.

When you see a billboard or any other public service announcement for helping kids, just think about a daily twinkle from a pair of big brown eyes that will always make you smile. Then, if you can, call your local department of children's services and find out how you can give a child a home. If it's a drug-addicted child, know that you're a foot soldier in a war that was never really fought and that most certainly made no provisions for prisoners.

NO EASTER BUNNIES HERE

I didn't do much about Easter when Brandi was little. She was too young to understand the religious meaning and even when she was almost two, she was still not old enough (developmentally) to enjoy the children's version of the celebration.

A new dress? I saw a lot of pretty little pastels on racks in stores in the toddler section that I suppose a lot of mothers chose from. But my little one would pull at her clothes until they had holes and came apart. And she hated to have certain fabrics next to her skin, and we never knew which fabric it would be.

A basket? I simply ignored the aisles where they were stacked and filled with goodies. If given to her, my girl would have dumped all the items out and thrown them everywhere.

A long time ago, when my daughters who are now grown lived at home, my Singer sewing machine buzzed into the late-night hours helping to produce years and years of Easter outfits.

And our baskets back then? They became a family enterprise. As those daughters grew older, they gave baskets to each other. Prizes were awarded for the one with the most creative contents— no eggs and no candy were the only rules.

But those traditional festivities didn't happen at my house for Brandi. In fact, as invitations arrived for Easter egg hunts others were having, I called in our regrets.

I could at least have bought her a pair of shoes, I kept telling myself. Or why didn't I buy a plush new stuffed toy? Why not a fluffy white rabbit, a soft yellow chicken, a duck, or any of the other stuffed animals that were sitting on the shelves at florists and bookstores?

And why didn't I at least buy a pair of shoes for this special day, since Brandi's last new shoes brought so much joy the adult members of my family say they will never forget her excitement?

For days after that purchase, she walked around constantly extending one foot and then the other one high into the air.

Her eyes were bright and wide—a sparkle that began at the shoe store. All the way back home she sat quietly in her carseat with eyes transfixed on her new acquisition.

She marched throughout the house to her own special cadence. By the end of that first day she had learned to say the word "shoe." She received great cheers and praise for her accomplishment.

When she'd meddle with things around the house that weren't touchables, I made the mistake of saying, while fanning my hands back and forth, "Shoo, shoo!"

"Shoe, shoe," she'd repeat and then lift her foot while pointing a small quivering finger in the direction of her treasure. (Whenever she is excited, and that's often, she quivers and sometimes that quiver goes into a tremendous amount of hard shaking.)

Three months after the shoo/shoe business, the word "shoe" was no longer part of her vocabulary. Maybe, as the experts suggest, it was forgotten. Crack babies have a pattern of slow and problematic language development.

Showing off her shoes changed too. The act was no longer a matter for praise. The shoes were now used for kicking, stomping, and throwing. And the kicking, stomping, and throwing would be what would have happened with the Easter basket whether it contained the traditional eggs and grass or the Smith kids' creative packaging.

There was a clinical reason for Brandi to spend a quiet Easter Sunday, and it's based on her mother using crack cocaine while pregnant. That drug, says the pediatric neurologist, affects the section of the brain that influences behavior.

The excitement of egg hunts, extra people, and new things weren't what my little one could handle right then. For although she was almost two years old, in many areas of development she tested at nine months.

Easter tradition? Not recommended for many of cocaine's youngest victims.

TRINKETS ON THE TREE

With Brandi, celebrations had to be handled carefully. Squeals and yells brought in the Christmas season the year when she was three with her first sighting of "Lights! Lights!"

"Ooh," squealed my little one as she peeked out the window of her bedroom to see the bright lights on the neighbor's front porch.

Then she jumped up and down in ecstasy and excitement. "They are so bea-u-ti-ful," she yelled while turning to me and pointing to the giant ten-foot palm tree house plant filling up one of the corners in our front room.

"Let's put some little lights on this one," she yelled even louder. Not a bad idea, I thought quickly. It would be quite festive, while at the same time allowing me to escape the traditional Christmas stuff.

"She's a girl after my own heart," I grinned to myself with inward delight. But as the days passed, I had an eerie feeling about my little one's unimposing request.

Each morning when we passed the wonderful smelling pine tree in the hallway at her pre-school and she stopped to admire the decorations and inhale the fresh aroma, I'd think, "She really knows about Christmas."

But each day when we drove back home in the evening by way of our local Christmas Tree Lane, and as she shouted at the lights in a loud and raucous voice, I would say to myself, "She's still overwhelmed by it all."

She brought home the decorations she made at school and shrieked and quivered with excitement while asking for something to put them in. I gave her a big green basket. She spent an endless amount of time arranging, and then rearranging, her handmade crafts.

And that year—because her ability to function with noise, people, and a lot of activity had shown improvement—we attended a few Christmas parties.

Brandi tuned them out. It was like she wasn't there. Even the party with Santa didn't get her attention because she was already focused on a chocolate cookie when the fat, bearded guy made his entrance.

But then came the ultimate party of all parties. This was the one we had to rehearse for. It wasn't a kiddie function, but it was something I knew she shouldn't miss.

"Now, there will be lots and lots of decorations everywhere," I preached, and then of course added, "There will be plenty to see, but not to touch."

"Plenty to see, but not to touch," she would repeat and then ask if it was okay to smell.

A fair trade, I reasoned, so I agreed to the nose thing, although it was probably frowned upon in polite circles.

Brandi was all aglow when the big night came. The decorations at the party were beyond our little rehearsals. Upstairs in the master bedroom, there was a great Christmas tree, stockings hanging by the fireplace, and a big antique trunk filled with more Pooh bears than she could think about counting—but she got to touch them.

One of the bathrooms in the house featured a huge Santa with reindeer and the other bath had a wonderful locomotive filled with Christmas trinkets. There was another gorgeous tree in the living room. There my girl also spotted an antique tricycle and a hobby horse.

Christmas was everywhere. In every corner. We didn't stay long but the evening left an impression.

Brandi was shaking with excitement when she arrived back home, and it took much longer than usual to calm her back down and bring her into focus. But she had handled the evening well.

Things that had been introduced at school came alive for her in a home setting. She realized that the Christmas spirit belonged everywhere, and I suspected she was ready for it to come to her house too.

The next day we bought a tree. She took all her decorations and other stuff, too, from her green basket and hung them on the branches. The basket was also hung on the tree. She took them off and put them back on. And she did that again and again.

I even brought out my tree trimmings that had been packed away from years gone by. The lights still worked. We strung them around the little tree instead of putting them on the living room plant.

Brandi adjusted to the holiday season that year. Still, it was hard for her—as it is for many other crack babies—to be part of what the rest of us see as an ordinary celebration. Most of us take the lights and trees, the Santas and reindeer, the music and the food, and the visitors and their gifts for granted. But for little ones who have to work very hard to keep their life on balance due to prenatal exposure to drugs, the season, like everything else for them, has to be introduced in a very gradual manner.

Education—
Who's Learning What?

PARENTS NEED TO BE INVOLVED

Only thirteen years ago, parents enrolled their daughter, let's call her Deanna, in a quaint, picturesque little elementary school that sat just down the block from where the family lived. Deanna was dressed in a plaid jumper, long socks, tennis shoes, and a hand-me-down white blouse.

For the first six years of the child's school experience, most things went well. The girl never got into any real trouble. That is, the parents say they were never required to come to the school.

Twice during those first six years they went to the open house, and each year they faithfully attended parent conferences. They once told a neighbor they had a "darn good record of involvement for such a long stretch of time."

Deanna never asked for help with her school work, and the parents never thought to ask if she needed any. Since report cards indicated she was an average student, if a D happened to appear, the parents simply told their daughter she needed to be more serious about her work.

For these parents, the secondary school years were basically a repeat of the elementary ones; no real trouble, no requirements, and, according to them, a "darn good record of involvement."

But by this time mother was working and father was holding down two jobs. When either of them was away from work in the evening, they wanted to enjoy the luxuries their additional income was affording them, and so parent conferences and open houses got left by the wayside.

It was a simple matter, they reasoned. The children, Deanna and her brother, were young adults now, and in their opinion part of being a responsible young adult meant knowing what the school and each individual class required.

Deanna still wasn't asking for any kind of help or guidance, and the parents, of course, weren't giving any. But Deanna did always ask to go shopping. Although this wasn't a family that was well off—in fact it was a family who struggled to make ends meet—the parents felt Deanna should have the best, and so the credit cards and checkbook were always hers for the asking.

Then came the June when Deanna was to graduate. All the years of shopping and forgetting about education came to a peak. It was the month of reckoning.

Deanna bought an expensive gown for the prom and all the necessary accessories. Then there was the senior class luncheon, announcements, cap and gown rental, pictures, ring, pin, grad night, picnic outfits, and other miscellaneous expenses.

Deanna hadn't acquired much knowledge. She hadn't learned to read very well, and her spelling was just as bad. Deanna didn't know what it meant to reason or apply a formula when a problem needed to be solved.

Mother and father were both upset when the counselor said their daughter didn't have the requirements for graduation. They were perplexed and seemed not to understand that credit cards and checkbook shopping were not what was needed.

What if the parents had become involved with the education process way back when mother didn't work and while Deanna was still wearing hand-me-down clothes?

Too many parents are too busy. And too many too busy parents can be heard saying, "We gave them everything they wanted. Where did we go wrong?"

TESTING, TESTING, 1, 2, 3

The clamor about school test scores is puzzling. If the purpose of educational testing is to determine where the individual student's weak spots are and then provide the needed assistance, then hooray! But that approach wouldn't get much attention because only parents would be notified of their child's individual results, and a counselor would then be assigned to help work out a remedy for the low score.

Shouldn't parents already have a pretty clear idea of their kids' academic levels prior to any testing? Shouldn't parents know this because they've been assisting at home?

Unfortunately, this often isn't the case. Many moms and dads are too busy working to pay for the trinkets that life in America has told them they need to have.

When parents purchase a new car, they carefully read the owner's manual to find out how the expensive buggy operates. They make sure to take it to the dealer for proper servicing and maintenance. They are very concerned about the warranty, and they make sure their insurance coverage for the vehicle is adequate.

On any given weekend, depending on the weather and the wallet, dad can be seen on the front lawn or at the car wash cleaning and polishing his newly acquired pride and joy.

Mom can be found at the beauty salon waiting patiently for her nail fills or a new set of artificial ones. From there, she'll make it to the gym for a workout, and late that evening she and dad will have an evening out.

The kids? Oh, they'll go shopping at the mall or hang out with their friends renting movies or throwing a small party poolside or in the hot tub area.

And during the week? Mom is tired when she comes home from work and dad is always at the office late. The kids watch television in their separate bedrooms, talk on the telephone, and play computer games. When it's time to eat, if they're teenagers, they jump in their cars and choose between McDonald's, Jack in the Box, and Burger King.

If they're too young to drive, they snatch a couple of sodas from the fridge, grab a TV dinner and pop it into the microwave, and enjoy cartoons or the company of a telephone dinner friend while they consume a lot of the bad stuff nutritionists are always warning against.

There aren't any books in the home, but there is an expensive giant screen TV and other elaborate components in the entertainment center located in the family room.

In this home, that is everywhere across America, there are few opportunities for expression of thought, no real discussions about issues, and that just might be why there is such a clamor for high test scores—since families themselves aren't producing any real measuring tools.

PROMS COST TOO MUCH

The story doesn't change. Oh, the details may vary, but the story is the same. The girl's name is different. The flowers that get ordered from the local florist have various aromas. Maybe they're orchids. Maybe they're roses. It doesn't really matter. The color and style of the dress, the name of the escort, and the place for the prom differ—but the story is the same.

To hear the plans for high school proms, it sounds like households with teenage kids have struck oil, found a gold mine, or invested in stock that has skyrocketed. Standard expenses for these events now include high cost tickets for dinner and dancing at a fancy upscale hotel, expensive ball gowns for the girls and rented tuxedos for their escorts, and extravagant after-prom parties and stretch limousines.

Of course, the young ladies have to keep shopping even after the purchase of the great gown. There has to be a classy wrap to ward off the chill of the night air. There has to be a proper necklace and earrings to match. New shoes are a must! And then there's hair, nails, and the growing need to spend the day of the prom at a spa to gain that very special glow!

Someone needs to put a stop to this behavior. First, schools are wrong to allow proms to be held at expensive places. Second, parents need to examine their values and their budgets. Oh, I've been called a party pooper before. And that may well be a very accurate name, because if I had my way, these end-of-the-year galas would be held in the school cafeteria or gymnasium that was beautifully decorated by theater arts and art department students. But fortunately, for those who are willing to put up money for a night of elegance, the power is in their hands and not mine.

Should I live and let live? As a writer, don't I have a social responsibility? If each of us lived by our own values and priorities and never voiced our opinion, how would we hear something different and then be able to question and examine our own scheme of existence?

I do live and let live. I have many friends and know many people who run their overextended credit cards to the max just to make prom night a memorable occasion. That's their choice. I make no comment. I have four daughters who did not participate in these heavy expenditures. That was our choice as a family, and we heard no comments.

But it would be socially irresponsible for me not to question the kind of money that is spent for a ride to a ball in a pumpkin that is rented on a credit card whose payment is already past due.

CLOTHES DON'T
MAKE THE STUDENT

Wearing a velveteen jumper, a white ruffled blouse, white tights with embossed designs, brocade pumps, and an elaborate hairstyle, the graduating middle-school student said to her mother as they left campus after the traditional summertime rite of passage ceremony, "You can tell the white parents don't really care about their kids; look how they're dressed."

Generally speaking, clothing for the day, indeed, could have been separated on ethnic lines as the young lady had observed; white students were casual, black students and their Latino counterparts were, for the most part, albeit in varying degrees, dressed to the nines. What's going on here?

Should it be determined that kids are products of non-caring parents if they wear jeans and a T-shirt to their school's final ceremony? And conversely, when school's opening bell rings will those students decked in the finest of young people's wear be representing the parents who care the most?

"Naw, naw, you just don't understand," begged the frustrated ninth-grader who was trying to convince the adults in his family that $55 shirts weren't too expensive for him to wear to high school. As a member of the school basketball team, the young man's family had already forked up lots of money for his required game shoes and other expenses.

"It's not really a polo shirt if it doesn't have the little horse logo," he explained several days later while grinning and pointing to the red horse on the left side of his newly acquired shirt.

"This is what everybody's wearing," said the kid who shouldn't have gotten his way.

What kids wear to school says a lot about the parents who pay the bills. But the cost of outfits doesn't say anything about the family income because credit cards have taken away the old common-sense budget phrase, "We can't afford it."

"You're wrong, absolutely wrong, if you think clothes don't make the difference in who I am," said the high school senior who had worked all summer to purchase her own clothes because her single mom couldn't afford (and didn't have any credit) to buy the brand names she insisted upon having.

No, the student hadn't been required to contribute any of her summer earnings to help meet the household expenses. Ms. Senior had gone to work, she explained several times, for the sole purpose of buying expensive clothes. And, yes, she insisted she knew about budgeting because she didn't have nearly enough with her earnings and with what her mother had given her to purchase all the clothing and accessory items she needed. So she had been forced to make some very critical decisions.

"Think of all those people who drive new cars, Ms. Smith. I just have clothes," she said rather curtly.

Why does her mother allow her daughter to live far beyond both of their financial means? Why doesn't mom teach some lessons here about how clothes don't really make the woman?

The answer is simple. Mom doesn't see anything wrong with living beyond what the paycheck dictates, and mom probably supports the theory that clothes make the woman.

"He's in the third grade and he doesn't care what he wears. He could leave any morning for school in shoes that don't match, and he would never notice, even if some other kids pointed it out," said one father who didn't exactly know what to make of his young son's cavalier attitude about clothes.

Another parent says her pre-schooler insists on laying out her clothes the night before and is very conscious of what she wears, what other people wear, and of how she is treated, which, she says, is based on how she looks.

Our children reflect the social attitudes they are surrounded with—and the emphasis in America is on spending and on how we look.

All too often, who we are is related to what we have. We can't judge which parents care the most by what their kids are wearing. Those in plain clothes at graduation just may be the ones whose families established college tuition plans long before their children could walk.

NO GIFTS FOR GRADS

"What to Give the Graduate" was the topic of my presentation to a large group of parents one night. After questions were answered and refreshments had been served, a kindly looking woman came to me, took me by the arm, and guided me out of the assembly room and into an empty hallway.

"I wanted to discuss this with you away from those parents who appeared"—and she heavily emphasized the word "appeared"—"to enjoy what you had to say." Her kindly demeanor had disappeared. Anger and frustration took over.

"Graduation is a time for celebration. It's a time to let our kids know that we are really proud of them," she said taking a deep breath and then continuing. "You hate your kids and all kids so much you would dare suggest we stop giving gifts."

My, uh, fan, with tears welling in her eyes and arms folded tightly against her chest, glared steadily at me. She told me how sorry she felt for kids I had already raised and said it was heartbreaking to know I was now a foster parent to a young child.

Why hadn't she raised the issue during the question and answer discussion?

"People were laughing and pretending to enjoy and to give thought to what you had to say, and you have a way of defending the non-caring philosophy you preach," she replied.

"I did ask a question," she said while wiping her tears and walking away. "You answered me, but you tried to make your answer sound like it made sense."

Her question from the floor had been: "If you don't think graduates expect and should receive the best gift we as parents can give them, do you really think you're in touch with reality?"

In the hallway, she explained it was the kindest way she could think of for letting me know I didn't know what I was talking about.

Here's what I was talking about: If we have been the right kind of parent, by the time our children step to the podium to receive their diploma, we have already given them the best of all gifts.

Were you there to help with the homework over the years? Were you aware of the assignments that were completed and the grades earned for various class projects? Where were you when it was your turn to drive the kids to Little League games?

When it came to problem matters, did you listen to the whole story and judge fairly whether your kid was in the right or in the wrong? Did you meet with teachers, counselors, and administrators when that was necessary for your kid's academic and social progress?

Throughout the years, did you stay abreast of the school's academic requirements? What kind of values and standards did you set? Was education an important goal? What kind of personal and family examples did you set?

If learning is a personal goal and achievement is a valued virtue, both graduate and parent are rewarded at graduation time.

I'm not as unrealistic as the lady in the hallway had hoped to make my audience believe. In America, life seems to be a lot of glitter and tinsel. If we are ever to rise above the superficial, it's going to have to start at home.

What About College?

I didn't have to make a dress. I didn't have to help her shop for shoes. I didn't even have to drop off or pick up from the hair appointment. I didn't have to inform friends and relatives. In fact, I didn't have anything to do but get there.

I wasn't involved with the classes she completed. I don't know what classes she dropped. I don't know how many days she was absent, and I don't know anything about assignments missed or exams that were failed.

I do know she said she never wanted to go to college. She said she just wanted to graduate from high school, get a job, and move away from my house (as soon as possible). I had some comments on that, but I was the mom and she was the daughter. It was her future, and she had finally reached the age where the decisions were all hers.

After high school graduation she got what she thought was a good job. She liked the work, but being a typist, she wasn't making very much money. Being an ambitious young lady, she decided to work two jobs. Her monthly income increased, but things still weren't quite right, she said.

She packed up, moved to Washington, D.C., and quickly found employment with much better pay and an impressive amount of responsibility. She was enthralled with the firm she worked for, but very soon she complained that things still weren't quite right. She said something was missing.

My Peggy liked what she was doing, and she liked the people she was doing it for. Her boss liked her work, and she was promoted within her first three months on the job. Something wasn't right, though. She said there was too much she didn't know. So, after her eight hours of work every day, she headed to the campus of the local junior college where she enrolled in a few business classes.

The classes were just what she needed—they let her know she needed a whole lot more!

Peggy soon moved back to the west coast and enrolled in San Francisco State University. She graduated with a B.A. in business management.

Graduation was a lot different this time around. This time I wasn't hand-stitching a hem on a dress from a Vogue pattern two hours before she was to march with the other high school seniors. This time around she shopped on her own. When I saw her after the ceremony, she was wearing a very chic black business suit underneath her graduation robe.

It wasn't my job to determine who would receive graduation announcements. I was consulted, but that was as far as it went. Everyone who should have been notified may or may not have been, but it wasn't up to me.

High school graduation is a time of beginning rather than ending. If graduates take a look at what they have gained, they know there is much more to acquire. If parents will give their kids the opportunity and support to explore their individual insights, limitations, interests, and talents, my experience says the long-run results will measure up to your expectations. My experience says the decision belongs to the graduate who should seek higher education only when they are ready for it.

Children Deserve the Best

BABIES HAVING BABIES

She opened all the baby shower gifts. There were the usual items: pink and blue knitted footwear, cute little sweaters with matching caps, blankets for crib and baby buggy, and smaller blankets for wrapping baby up tight.

There were gowns and diaper sets, and someone even gave the mother-to-be a three-month gift certificate for a diaper service.

The guests and the lady of honor played the regular baby shower games.

The party ended and the guests left and went their separate ways.

The mother-to-be put her baby gifts back in their individual boxes. She collected ribbons and other mementos to later display in the baby book she had received that day.

After thanking the hostess for the shower, the lady of honor—the mother-to-be—with the help of her own mother and two younger sisters, put the gifts into their car and drove home.

The lady of honor was sixteen, and she was impressed with the afternoon event—so were her sisters, ages thirteen and fourteen.

On the ride home, the young sisters said they were envious because big sis had been the center of attention. They also said they loved the soft pastel baby clothes and the cute cuddly stuffed toys their sister had received as gifts.

Each one managed to proclaim her intent to follow the impressive pattern set by big sis.

And it was an impressive pattern, for not only had big sis been the center of attention on this day, but she had also managed during the past eight months to keep up all of her social contacts and obligations.

Although she had gained an excessive amount of weight and therefore no longer fit into her stylish tight-fitting designer jeans, and although her feet were frequently swollen and her high heel shoes didn't fit very well, she still managed to attend the local Friday and Saturday night foot-stomping events.

Seemingly, younger sisters and the young mother-to-be don't know what becoming a mother actually involves.

With all the frivolity, with all the pink and blue ribbons, with all the thoughts spent on naming the new baby, with the shopping for clothes and furniture and all the weekend parties, there was no time devoted to the serious side of motherhood.

Where is the someone who can convince these young unmarried "babies" who are having babies that motherhood is a difficult task requiring maturity, direction, and the shared involvement of the male parent?

Is there someone who can convince these young teenagers that after the baby shower and after the labor pains comes the day-to-day responsibility that's required of mothers for eighteen years and more?

CUTIE IN A BONNET

Calling all older mothers! Grab the hot-to-trot teenyboppers who think babies are cute little baby dolls and give these girls a chance to walk a few miles in your shoes.

Find a bunch of young maidens who need something to call their own. Bring forth the thirteen-year-olds who need love. Get a room crowded full of them, who the experts say need something to brag about, and give 'em a glimpse of their future.

Motherhood, whether you're fourteen or forty, means you no longer have a life.

The first clue to this condition is the zombie-like existence that develops due to lack of sleep, and that begins immediately after returning from the birth center or maternity ward.

Now, this lecture won't be for the teenagers whose mothers are foolish enough to take on the care of the new bundle of questionable joy. Instead, these words are for those little girls who should still be playing jump rope and paper dolls but who are awakening every morning at 2 a.m. to feed a wailing baby and to change a poopy diaper.

Sex may have been fun, but the aftermath isn't. Whoever the boy was who shared the pleasure, he isn't there now for his end of the responsibility.

Tell these girls their life is going to be a voyage on mighty rough waters called single parenting.

There are bottles to be washed (or purchased and thrown away), shopping to be done, well-baby clinic appointments to be made and to be kept.

Colds, measles, mumps, and chickenpox will visit their household. High temperatures have to be cared for and brought back down to normal. There's also the great discomfort for mother and child alike when teething comes to visit, again and again.

Children seem to never stop crying. And as mom walks the floor frustrated and ineffective, when it comes to soothing the childhood aches, she'll be crying too.

Though these are just a few of the smaller parental headaches and inconveniences, they're enough to make any sailor seasick.

Both motherhood and single parenting navigate on some mighty rough waters.

Remind these young girls that they will soon stop talking about how cute their little one is when they hold it and talk to it and it makes baby sounds and smiles.

And when their friends gather around to admire the little one's new bonnet with the matching sweater and blanket, remind them that the quick burst of pride they experience is short-lived.

Most important, please remind them when their new boyfriend starts telling them how good they look and how he wants them to have his baby, that they've heard that line before.

Mothers who have been there and done that, please help these girls understand that the baby's cute smile, the compliments coming from friends, and the new boyfriend's line of crap have nothing to do with them as a person, a woman, or a mother.

All mothers need a life. The world is bigger than strollers, cribs, Similac, Gerbers, and Toys R Us. From those who have been there, we'll tell you: a baby is a hard ship for a teenager to steer.

Kool-Aid vs. Fruit Juice

"You won't have to give her any dinner tonight because she stuffed herself at McDonald's on a cheeseburger—pickles and everything," said the proud aunt when, after an all-day outing, she returned her niece home to mom and dad.

Mom went into quick shock at the news of a twelve-month-old being fed at the famous Golden Arches.

"McDonald's?" mom stammered, while staring with a strained and searching gaze into the eager and wanting-to-please bright eyes of the aunt from Chicago.

It was then, mom said, that auntie, perhaps feeling she had not said enough to be impressive about the day's activities, added the horrifying addendum concerning the pickles and other trimmings.

As mom told this tale to other people, she admitted she was plain and simple knocked for a loop. It had never occurred to her, she said, that anyone would do such a thing.

It didn't take mom long to find out a whole bunch of people make the same kind of food choices for their young.

There was a nine-month-old baby she soon heard about. His mother said, "We don't feed him any baby food, he just won't eat it. He eats whatever we do, and that is usually hamburgers with fries."

And with the utmost calm, this baby's mother delivered the clincher. "He just loves chocolate. Whenever we give him anything chocolate—cookies, candy, cake, anything—he just naturally freaks out."

The shocked mom also heard about the baby who was three weeks old and drinking Kool-Aid. The parents of this little one said it was time for their infant to have a little fruit juice between regular feedings.

When asked why they selected Kool-Aid, the mother hastily responded, "It's what my mother always gave her babies."

There was a food story from a CPR class in which the instructor, who was a paramedic, told of answering 911 calls because of babies choking after being fed hot dogs. Then there are the babies at the movies who are fed popcorn, Coke, and 7Up while their parents sip, munch, and stare at the big screen.

Why do people feed babies bad stuff?

The answer could be quite simple: they don't know any better.

But isn't the public constantly told about the virtues of vegetables, fruits, dairy products, whole grain cereals, and beans?

Is there a jingle that says a Big Mac a day will keep the doctor away? (We've heard an apple will.)

Do Kool-Aid commercials give us a clever jingle claiming their liquid sugar is fruit juice?

How did chocolate become a preferred between-meal snack for baby when every pediatrician and all other health practitioners involved with young children and their parents stress proper nutrition?

Nutritionists have an important, straightforward, and simple message.

Neither popcorn nor peanuts should be given to children under two years of age because they can't chew them correctly, and because they can be inhaled into their lungs.

Beans are an excellent source of protein without the high fat and sodium content found in hamburgers.

If parents counted the cost of hot dogs, luncheon meat, and hamburgers ounce for ounce, they would find the price is quite high. Beans are much less expensive.

On the matter of soda and other flavored sweet water, their high sugar content and total lack of nutritional value means they have not much reason for being. Giving these foods to a small child is like giving them two cups of coffee. It keeps them going with an artificially high level of activity, and it influences their behavior and sleep patterns.

That's what the professionals say, but unfortunately, not enough parents are listening.

Just a Housewife

The young teenager said she wanted to be a wife and mother when she grew up. The room grew silent. Everyone waited for more. Nothing else was said. The attractive young girl lowered her eyes, smiled at her mother, and left the room.

"But doesn't she want to go to college?" asked one of the career women guests, who was attending a women's get-together at the house of the teenager's mother.

Another visitor remembered that the last time she had talked with the girl she had been interested in a theatrical career. "She worked long and hard, I remember," said the second guest. "Is she really going to give all of that up without even making the big time?"

"Oh, don't get carried away or worried," remarked another guest. "With her mother's influence and the way kids change, she'll come to her senses."

The rest of the evening these dynamic career women talked of their success on the job and their new abilities to call their own shots, and they projected into the future.

No recipes were exchanged, few comments were made about husbands, and almost all of them forgot to talk about their children. Well, they did criticize the hostess for having a daughter with low expectations.

Women of today? No one could call them old-fashioned!

Once upon a time it was quite appropriate for girls to want a life as wife and mother. That was a long, long time ago.

What's the matter with being called a housewife and what's the matter with changing dirty diapers? Women used to do those things: they tended the house and the children, and they didn't feel less because of it.

The women who tend their homes and take care of their children on a full-time basis in conversation often say, "I'm just a housewife." Just a housewife?

The career women workshops and the job-after-middle-age career centers have been busy rewording that concept. They have taken great steps in organizing proper language to describe the financial management, secretarial output, psychological counseling, and other job-related functions the wife and mother perform at home.

This updated language may have its main audience among women just entering the workforce, but for those still at home doing the wash, they don't think of it as laundry service, and they don't see paying the bills as financial management. Picking up the kids and running errands isn't called scheduling.

For the women who still prepare their children's breakfast and nurse them when they're sick, they're doing the most important job there is. Without women like the young lady who disappointed her mother's upwardly mobile associates by saying her career aspirations were to be a wife and mother, the career mothers of the future would be without a good neighbor to look after their kids while they attend the late evening corporate board meeting.

CHILDREN'S DAY

When I was a little girl, I frequently asked my mother why there wasn't a children's day since mothers and fathers each had a day for celebration.

My mother's answer, like most of her responses to my childhood queries, was right to the point. "There's no special Children's Day," she said, "because children's day is every day."

That was a good enough answer for me. Yes, it made sense. My world at that time was quite small. It consisted of my family, my parents' circle of friends, and my friends in elementary school who were also the neighborhood kids. And from my young and narrow vantage point, children had a special place in the lives of the people they interacted with.

It made sense to me that parents would need a special day. All the other days in the year I saw them devote an immeasurable amount of time to the care and upbringing of their young.

But what I believed way back then is far from the reality in the new millennium. Nowadays, families can't be relied upon to be the protectors of their young. Neighborhoods are no longer support systems for children. It is now necessary for a multitude of social service agencies to act on behalf of children.

Thousands of child abuse and neglect cases are reported to authorities on a yearly basis. And of course there are the multitude of cases which go undetected. Much of this abuse occurs within the family, and many children die as a result of these incidents.

Children bear the brunt of adult frustration. Neglect and maltreatment, which are classified as abuse, are often so subtle they aren't easily recognized or detected by family members or authorities, and lack of food, housing, warm clothing, or proper medical treatment isn't even in this category.

Child neglect is easy to pinpoint when the headlines carry a story about a mother who has left her new baby at home unattended for several days while she's gone somewhere doing drugs. The baby is dead when she returns, and mom doesn't even remember leaving. There are also the stories that are brought to the public's attention about emaciated children whose parents have kept them locked up for years in a closet or in a small dark room.

But the public doesn't hear about the subtle kind of abuse people often witness but for some reason choose to look the other way. This is the kind we witness on an individual basis and never talk about. These maltreatments are the kind we might observe even at a friend's house, and then later tell ourselves our observation wasn't what our gut reaction said it was.

Families reflect the conditions of the environment in which they live. Parents generally raise their kids the way they were raised. Children are raised in an atmosphere that depends on how the adults they are with interpret the world in which they live.

All too often adult experiences aren't those that should be passed on to the children. How many bad days turn into nightmares for children who are unable to defend themselves against an irate older person? How many nightmares are inflicted upon children because the adult in charge thought they could teach the youngster a lesson they would never forget?

At a workshop session, a very sincere parent said, "I told my five-year-old not to take the plate out of the oven because it was hot and would burn her, but she took it out anyway and got burned. What kind of punishment would you recommend?"

The workshop leader managed to keep a straight face, passed no judgmental answer, and simply said, "It would seem the burn she received was enough to help your little girl understand not to touch when she is told something is hot."

The parent didn't take the conversation any further, but she in fact had punished the youngster much further and very severely.

Isn't it okay to gently question a friend or relative who seems pretty close to crossing the border from discipline to abuse? A little conversation can go a long way in correcting subtle maltreatment. Sometimes folks just don't know any better. They've never had the privilege of knowing matters can be handled in another way.

Times have changed plenty since I was a little girl, or maybe my horizons have simply broadened. But my mother had the right idea—Children's Day should be every day.

Every Step Needs a
Helping Hand

Remember baby's first steps? Oh, how they sort of hesitate just before take-off. Mom or pop, or one of the older kids in the family, stands there with outstretched arms urging the toddler on. And remember that eager look as baby looks from face to face and waddles off in the direction of a pair of outstretched arms, headed for what maybe the kid perceives as the most encouraging look or voice?

Sometimes the toddler doesn't quite make it on the first go 'round, when the excitement and his underdeveloped coordination trip him up. But the arms of support and the words of encouragement are there for the next attempt.

Pediatricians always want to know when a baby learned to walk. And for those who have baby books, you will indeed find the date of a very first step.

Taking steps, whether baby ones or giant ones, continues throughout life, all along our path of achievement. These steps mark the milestones of our journey upward.

But there are some babies who are left alone without any onlookers to encourage them. They take off and experience their very first step all alone. They too stumble, maybe even fall, but they get up on their own and do, indeed, eventually learn to walk.

There is no record in their baby book. And, after all, the pediatrician doesn't need to know the exact date of this first step; it's really only important to know the month. And even the parents who aren't there with outstretched arms have a close enough clue to this.

Some parents fail to realize their children keep on taking steps, and every one of the steps needs encouragement. Those funny looking pictures coming home from grade school need to be hung

in a place of honor in the home. Those glee club and school productions must be attended by parents or another adult relative.

Too many of our children accept the underachieving role their
parents have helped them attain. And even though these parents
never took the time or had the interest to watch their babies learning to walk and other important events along the way, they will be
found in later years sitting in the front row of the courtroom as the
judge passes sentence and makes the determination as to which
step their kid will take next.

INTERPRETING LIFE

There is a powerful burden on the shoulders of America's black parents. Throughout our existence, in this land called home, it has been our responsibility to interpret life and pass it on to our young. That is no different from the responsibility of parents in other cultures. But our responsibility is burdensome because we must prepare our offspring for an environment that awaits them with folded arms of indifference, pale images, and empty promises. Ours is an awesome task for, as we prepare our young for the challenge ahead, our blackness must be developed in a positive force; but at the same time we must also interpret for our young the racism that permeates the land.

We must teach constantly that blackness is beautiful. We must surround our young with supportive images of themselves and of the people of earlier generations. We must make and keep the folklore of black America as an integral part of our everyday existence.

While we prepare our young to appreciate history and blackness, we must also teach them, as our Native American brothers and sisters might put it, "the ways of the white man." Although a historical overview is best for a full understanding of American racism, for our young, an honest explanation of what is happening in their day-to-day existence is excellent transition material.

But we must be honest and face the fact that much of this historical information is ignored, and the truth is that too many black people just don't want to hear about yesterday.

My mother talked often about her great grandmother who was twelve when she was freed from slavery. No one in the family would listen to Granma's stories about life on the plantation. Granma was always told, "nobody wants to hear all 'bout that stuff." So, in ten years of living with an integral part of her history, my mother learned only that Granma had lived in "the big house," that she had been educated, and that the master's family had been very kind.

Years later, as a grandmother herself, my mother returned to Austin, Texas, with two of my children. Mom spent a lot of time with the old folks of the family, some of whom were in their late 90s. She learned a lot of history, but her grandchildren—my children—learned very little. They were left with other relatives while my mother visited the old folks.

I was disappointed, but when my mother and I sat down to talk and she unfolded years of family history, much of which she had never known, I learned that so much of black folks' lives is painful that they feel they cannot lay that burden on the young.

That is not to say that all our lives, or all aspects of our lives, are painful. The point is that much of it hurts, and retelling it hurts, and sometimes we don't know if the people we tell will be hurt by it too. Sometimes if we talk about even the good times, and we keep on talking, we will say too much and reveal the skeletons that we think are in the closet. Sometimes it is simply that we are ashamed of the way things were.

After we have broken down our own barriers, black parents still face the task of interpreting white America for our young. Do we tell them that there is no place reserved for them in this great homeland of the free? Do we tell our sons that the penitentiary is holding their reservation, or our daughters that the street corners are holding theirs?

It is our responsibility to interpret America's blueprint for our young. But we must also become our own architects and draw up new plans. Yes, we tell our young about the road back to the "big house," to the penitentiary and the street corner. But we teach them and lead them to higher ground.

There Are No Bad Kids

WHERE ARE THE PARENTS?

It was Friday night. The kids, like a lot of other kids in a lot of other cities, towns, and hamlets all across America, were walking home from the local high school football game.

Which team won the game? Well, there's not much of a story in that common event. Football games are won or lost week after week and season after season.

But there was another game played that night. One without goal posts, referees, coaches, or uniforms.

The kids were heading home. It wasn't that late for a Friday night; it was just about 10 p.m., and the kids felt safe. They had walked the same route many times before. This was their regular way home after a football game.

But this night their familiar path took a sudden, irregular turn. There emerged from one of the neat little homes with the well-kept lawns several large and overpowering young men.

"Give up the money," one of the big guys from the house demanded.

"Don't move—we're going to empty your pockets," another member of the menacing group threatened.

The little boys, three of them, all under twelve years of age, did exactly as they were told.

The oldest one, who was exactly twelve, decided not to conform. He wanted, he later said, to stand up for his rights. He didn't like the idea of having his pockets picked.

After the younger boys were searched, released, and told to move on, the twelve-year-old was physically held by some members of the big guys' group while others beat and knocked him to the ground.

The thugs actually allowed the kid to keep his money, but that was only because they found his footwear to be a more attractive deal.

The victim kept his money, but lost his $150 Air Jordan basketball shoes. The thugs weren't all bad; one of them provided the victim with a pair of cheap sneakers right off his very own feet.

Where were the parents who lived in the house with the nicely groomed front lawn from which the thugs emerged?

Perhaps they were out for the evening and therefore missed the commotion in front of their home. But when they returned, was it their son who was wearing a pair of Air Jordans that hadn't been part of his wardrobe before they stepped out that night?

Perhaps the expensive shoes went to another house. But whoever the guy was who made the trade, chances are he took his stolen treasure into his parent's or other adult relative's home.

Thugs don't hatch from unattended eggs, nor do they drop from trees like overripe fruit. Thugs are raised by parents who don't understand they are supposed to tend the nest. Parental responsibility requires being in charge.

Neighborhoods haven't deteriorated; parental responsibility has. Thugs aren't taking over the streets; parents have given them their permission. Kids haven't gone bad; parents have.

WHO REALLY REGULATES TV?

The young mother always let her kids watch television. It didn't matter what the program was as long as the youngsters were happy, quiet, and out of her way.

As little babies they didn't yet have a personal television set of their own, so, at the age of one or two months, they were simply placed in the living room facing the boob tube, propped up in their little infant seats.

"They just love watching television," the mother said on one of those Saturday morning occasions. She said the babies would sit almost all day fascinated by the changing colors and pictures.

Saturday mornings were particularly painful in this household. The smallest baby, along with other older toddlers and pre-schoolers, would spend the early morning hours watching cartoons while sucking on Kool-Aid in bottles and spilling breakfast items all over the room. In a nearby bedroom, mom hid under her covers trying to catch the winks of sleep she'd missed the night before due to the hip-shaking party she'd attended until 3 a.m.

Her kids are older now. There's a television set in their bedrooms. No need for an infant seat anymore. The last kid who sat in one is now able to operate the remote control on his own.

Mom doesn't attend those late-night parties either. She now has a very good job and her future looks a lot brighter. She has a life. She doesn't feel so bogged down with children.

But ask what those kids of hers watch on their bedroom television and without hesitation she'll say she doesn't know. Ask about the amount of violence in their program choices, and she'll answer with a quizzical look that asks, "Does it matter?"

Some lawmakers and activists think so. Concerned about the psychological impact of violent programming on children, they've worked hard for a reduction of it. They say what is on the tube is directly related to the violence in our society.

Congressional hearings have produced talk of regulating the industry. Some of the networks offer a parental advisory plan that labels violence-prone shows with "Due to some violent content, parental discretion is advised."

How many kids are going to see the warning and say, "OOPS, not for me," and change the station? Zero.

How many parents are going to patrol the bedrooms on the hour and on the half hour to find out which programs have a warning? Very few.

What we need is nonviolent programs because too many parents don't have a clue as to what their kids are watching, and if they know, they don't see any harm being done. Today's young parents didn't have their viewing habits monitored when they were kids, so they don't see the need to provide that kind of supervision.

One of the children who, as a baby, used to fall asleep in his infant seat in front of the television was recently playing at a neighborhood park when gunfire erupted.

"That wasn't nothing," he said, when asked about the incident.

He was also asked, "Were you scared?"

"Uh, hum—sorta," he answered in a very detached manner.

For this little boy, the fracas at the park was just one more Saturday morning in front of the boob tube minus the breakfast stuff spilled everywhere.

STOLEN GOODS: BRING 'EM HOME

How many parents will receive from their offspring the gift of all gifts? Presents so costly that not even in prosperous years would the parents have imagined anyone they knew being able to afford such things.

"For me?" they will shriek in unison as they open package after package. The "oohs" and "aahs" will be echoed by the givers as they view and appraise the full array of items they've brought home.

So many presents will make the occasion seem like a birthday party or an anniversary celebration.

The first gift will be a brand new entertainment center for the living room. All the components will have been brought through the back door, during the night, by the kids and some of their friends who spent the evening, in what they declared, was an act of community liberation.

"Oh, baby, that's a nice one," mom coos as the muscular young men squeeze the giant piece of electronic furniture into a room almost too small for the 27-inch television set already sitting there on top of an upside-down orange crate.

Once everything is brought in, pops will rise from his easychair and help the young men set up the VCR, and all the other components that he knew existed but never had enough money to purchase.

"I'm not going to ask any questions," pops mutters. But his boys and their friends don't mind talking because they're impressed with the rhetoric.

"There's no justice in America."

"I don't have the money to buy things."

"The big boys and the politicians help themselves to what's out there!"

These and other justifications don't work. If parents allow kids to steal and bring the goods home, what lesson is being taught? How can parents teach children to be honest and to give respect while at the same time opening the back door to accept stolen merchandise? Of course there are parents, like pops, who prefer not to ask any questions and pretend they don't know where the merchandise comes from.

Then there will be the parents, like mom, who if asked will be quick to make up any kind of excuse. "Oh, his friend's family moved away and they gave our boy the stuff."

Parents have the major responsibility of preparing children for life. It is wrong to allow kids to steal. It is wrong to accept what they bring home. The cost of condoning this kind of behavior will never be rung up on the store's cash register, nor will it ever show on the monthly credit card statement. But in the long run, parents can rest assured the cost of jail time, court, and attorney's fees will measure out to be much more than the retail value of an entertainment center.

Just Say No

Parental involvement and ongoing supervision are mainstays when it comes to raising children who grow up to be productive citizens. To put it another way: parents need to know what their kids are up to.

Parents need to stop making excuses and instead be up-front about their children. Too many parents are receiving failing marks in the category of taking a good hard look at the kids and owning up to what they're raising. Parents are often in denial, and rather than handle the complexities that accompany this job, they simply allow the children to raise themselves.

That doesn't work. Kids should not be setting the rules and making the household decisions. Often, even the toddlers get to determine when it's bedtime and what will be served for breakfast.

But when the cute little toddler grows into a big ugly-acting teenager, the parents throw up their hands and ask, "What went wrong?"

Parents need to take charge in the early stages of their child's development, and the establishment of responsible communication must take place. It is important to share more with children than living space.

Children need parents they can talk with. That can start, some say, when the baby is still in the womb. There is so much more to providing for our offspring than holding down two full-time jobs to have enough income to be a better consumer.

Back in the days when common sense was the hallmark of parenting, parents had a handle on what their kids were up to. Back then, parents weren't worried about giving their kids everything on the wish list.

A long time ago parents weren't afraid to tell their kids NO without giving them an explanation for the answer, and those same old-time parents didn't regard the bedrooms in the house their children slept in as an area they, the parent, couldn't enter. Parents used to own the house and everything in it, including the very often surly and belligerent offspring.

Stock-piling ammunition, building pipe bombs, and connecting to violent or pornographic sites on the Internet can't happen when the warden (mom/pop) is in charge of every room—and everything in it. Invading kids' privacy is not to be confused with knowing what your kid is about.

The little kid in the neighborhood who breaks his pet bird's legs, punches his newborn baby brother on the ride home from the hospital, lies about everything including what happened to the missing parts of his bicycle, and kicks his best friend in the nose and tells him if he reports it to the teacher his fat neck will get broken, is headed for trouble. This same kid will grow up and pistol-whip the clerk in the store he's robbing. He, of course, will plead not guilty. His parents will say he didn't do it and might even take the witness stand to provide him with a false alibi. And these, of course, are the same parents who claimed the bird's leg was broken because it got caught in the cage door. These are the same parents who didn't believe their kid was a bully.

As television viewers we had the opportunity to see a young man caught on news footage grabbing a driver from the cab of his truck and brutally beating him during the 1992 Los Angeles riots. The mother of the young man was later heard outside the courthouse during her son's trial loudly proclaiming her boy's innocence.

Parents with a cover-up philosophy help create the monsters society has to incarcerate.

Children don't go bad on the day their crime takes place. These children, who lacked parental guidance, didn't just go bad the day after they blew out the candles on their teenage birthday cake.

Children aren't inherently bad. But what should be said about their parents?

BOTH SIDES OF THE TRACK

Barbara and Harold lived the good life. He earned a lot of money. She had her own career. They had a new house. They lived in the suburbs, and they were also parents.

Harold, the father, believed extramarital affairs were a good thing, because as he put it, "It keeps the wife on her toes."

Well, maybe not on her toes, but Harold's inability to be the husband Barbara wanted helped, she said, influence her drug habit.

"I realize it's all about me and my lack of coping skills," she said, and went on to say that if Harold spent time with her she thinks she wouldn't have become a substance abuser.

Barbara won her man back. In the by and by, Harold found that the cocaine his wife used as an escape tended to give him much more pleasure and satisfaction than the ladies of the night (and afternoon and breakfast hour) he had been keeping company with. The money he had been spending on prostitutes, women in the office, and "gals" at the bar started going to Barbara's dealer.

Better than the postal delivery service, the teenage dealer of Barbara's was always on time. This teenage dealer guy brought more than enough "white powder" product for Harold and Barbara.

There was a strange and compelling bond that now existed between the couple. Bad times were behind them. They were now committed—mainly to cocaine. They were now madly in love— more with cocaine than each other.

It never occurred to this very sad and misguided suburban couple that their lifestyle and contacts had a very deep influence on their children.

Michael, Barbara's seventeen-year-old son from a previous marriage, idolized the young dealer guy. This fascination had been brewing for several years.

As a graduation gift from elementary school, dealer guy introduced Michael to drugs. "No charge," he boasted, "your parents pay the bill."

Life wasn't any different for the other children of Barbara and Harold. Drugs were a way of all their lives. Drugs were an integral part of lavish parties, expensive cars, designer clothes, and smart friends. It was all part of the scene.

On the other side of the tracks, in one of the apartments located on the bottom floor of the city's urban housing project, Lela sat at the kitchen table with her arms folded across her broad bosom.

She's a single parent on welfare. Her check pays the rent, and if she carefully watches how the utilities are used, it sometimes can be stretched to cover them also.

Malcolm, her youngest, who is nine years old, just gave her money to buy groceries. He didn't give up all his cash because he planned on buying some flashy clothes for himself and another brother. Malcolm also wanted to give his sister enough to buy things for her new baby—in particular, a bed to sleep in.

Lela isn't into drugs, but her kids sure are. Her oldest boy, Tyrone, is doing time for selling. Marcus, the son who once did very well in school, got busted for possession. Kaisha, her only daughter, was an addict but got clean during her pregnancy. And Malcolm, the youngest of the brood? Well, he has contacts on the street that keep money in his pocket and food on his mother's table.

The school tells Lela that Malcolm is a slow learner and is hyperactive. But the youngster counts and manages money very well, and if his street teachers were to hear about his hyperactivity, they would laugh because he knows the customers and he knows where to be and exactly when to be there. He also knows how to look out for undercover cops, and he knows how to stash the drugs if he does get caught. Malcolm's weekly earnings suggest he learns some things very well.

Is Lela ashamed of her kids and the lifestyle they all live? Her husband went to prison when she was pregnant with Malcolm. She has been a faithful wife and has visited him through the years but doesn't believe he will ever walk the streets again.

She doesn't have a career. She doesn't have any job skills. Lela's lifestyle is quite a bit different from Harold and Barbara's, but then again, it is pretty much the same. Both families are in the same fix, and where they live or how much money they have doesn't matter. All across America, in the small towns, on the country roads, in upscale suburbia, and in the blighted inner city, drugs are leaving families crippled and torn.

Conclusion

Everywhere I go, I hear the same comment: "Our children are in trouble." Just about every parent I talk to, rich as well as poor, black as well as white, seems to have lost control.

However, there remains a handful of strong parents who have held on to the old-time teaching guidelines for raising children. Now it's time for this group to come together and prepare for battle.

There's a war to be fought and many battles to be won, and we can't leave this important struggle to our government, for it will surely be as bungled and lost as the war on drugs.

We have to save the children. Not just yours and not just mine. We have to save *all* children. We've got to bring back that old-time religion once known as parental responsibility. We're going to have to teach and preach the gospel everywhere we go, and we're going to need to talk to every parent we meet. We're going to stop pretending that rude and misbehaving children are okay and acceptable.

The Parent Brigade is going to tell it like it is. We're going to let it be known that children are becoming the parents and that the parents have learned to obey quite nicely.

We're going to stop watching the neighbor's teenagers unload explosives from the SUV while telling ourselves that what they do is their business.

All the children belong to all of us. The neighbor's misbehaving child is, when it comes to responsibility, our child. This war is one we can't afford to lose. Our battles will not be the kind where blood is shed, but instead we will fight for the purpose of sharing with others the strategies that work.

We're going to need every parent who has raised children to become productive adults with good character and a strong moral code of ethics to step up and enlist in this war.

Can we count on you?

Shirlee Smith with foster-daughter Brandi

Shirlee Smith writes about the principles that govern her old-fashioned, no-nonsense approach to parenting. A graduate of the University of California, Los Angeles, in 1972, she began her studies while raising five children. A former columnist for the *Pasadena Star News*, she frequently wrote about her "common sense" parenting methods. Currently, Smith is the host and producer of *Talk About Parenting*, a nationally-syndicated television program, and she also presents workshops and training sessions for parents.